Rethinking Am

★★★★★★★★★★★★★★★★★★★★★★★★★★★★★★

A High Intermediate
Cultural Reader

M. E. Sokolik
University of California, Berkeley

HH HEINLE & HEINLE PUBLISHERS
I(T)P™ *an International Thomson Publishing Company*

Boston – Albany – Bonn – Cincinnati – Detroit – London – Madrid –
Melbourne – Mexico City – New York – Pacific Grove – Paris –
San Francisco – Tokyo – Toronto – Washington

The publication of *Rethinking America 2, A High Intermediate Cultural Reader* was directed by members of the Newbury House ESL/EFL Team at Heinle & Heinle Publishers:

Erik Gundersen: Senior Editor, ESL/ELT
Charlotte Sturdy: Market Development Director
Mike Burggren: Production Services Coordinator
Stanley J. Galek: Vice President and Publisher

Also participating in the publication of this program were:
Managing Developmental Editor: Amy Lawler
Developmental Editor: John Chapman
Assistant Editor: Jill Kinkade
Manufacturing Coordinator: Mary Beth Hennebury
Project Manager/Interior Designer: Linda Dana Willis
Cover Designer: Gina Petti
Cover Artist: Andy Warhol
Compositor: Modern Graphics, Inc.
For permission to use copyrighted material, grateful acknowledgment is made to the copyright holders on the Credits page, which are hereby made part of this copyright page.

Pre-recorded material supplied by CNN. © 1999 Cable News Network, Inc. All rights reserved. © 1999 Turner Learning, Inc. All rights reserved.

ISBN: 0-8384-4741-4

Front cover illustration: Warhol, Andy (1928-87). Soup Can: Black Bean. Tate Gallery, London, Great Britain. The Andy Warhol Foundation, Inc./Art Resource, NY

ACKNOWLEDGMENTS

★★★

The fact that only my name appears on the cover seems a misrepresentation. Many, many people have helped in putting these volumes together. First and foremost, I would like to thank my Developmental Editor, John Chapman. His clarity of vision, insightful ideas, and masterful organization made this process much smoother than it otherwise would have been. Second, I would like to thank Erik Gundersen, Senior Editor, Heinle & Heinle for his unstinting support of the series and its expansion. I would also like to express my appreciation to Amy Lawler, Managing Developmental Editor, for doing such a great job in pulling all the pieces together and making sure everything was done right.

Other people at Heinle & Heinle have made valuable contributions as well. Joyce LaTulippe, Associate Developmental Editor, and Jonathan Boggs, Marketing Development Director, helped with the initial conception and development of the series. Jill Kinkade, Assistant Editor and Anne Sokolsky, Permissions Editor, dealt with the near-impossible task of getting rights to the authentic selections. And Becky Stovall, CNN Executive Producer in Atlanta, tracked down all the CNN video clips used in the series.

I also want to thank the reviewers and focus-group participants, whose insights and suggestions aided in the revision of the original text and in the conception of the two new volumes in the series:

Leslie Adams, Santa Ana College, CA

Alicia Aguirre, Cañada College, CA

Thom Allen, Chabot College, CA

Angelina Arellanes-Núñez, El Paso Community College, TX

Mardelle Azimi, California State University at Fullerton, CA

Victoria Badalamenti, LaGuardia Community College, NY

Gerald Lee Boyd, Northern Virginia Community College, VA

Pam Breyer, Braille Institute, CA

Mary Lou Byrne, Triton College, IL

Judi Camacho, Harper College, IL

Karen Carlson, Contra Costa College, CA

Jennifer Castello, Cañada College, CA

Anne Dorobis, Language Training Institute, NJ

Kathleen Flynn, Glendale Community College, CA

Ellen Clegg, ELS Language Center, CA

Patty Heiser, University of Washington Extension, WA

Jan Herwitz, ELS Language Center, San Francisco, CA

Gregory Keech, City College of San Francisco, CA

Julie Kim, University of Pennsylvania, PA

Tay Leslie, ELS Language Center, Los Angeles, CA

Kathleen Letellier, University of California Berkeley Extension, CA

Emily Lites, American Business English, CO

Robyn Mann, Harper College, IL

Roxanne Nuhaily, University of California, San Diego Extension, CA

Judith L. Paiva, Northern Virginia Community College, VA

Anita Razin, Santa Ana College, CA

Jan Rinaldi, Rio Hondo College, CA

Sandy Saldana, Triton College, IL

Irene Schoenberg, Hunter College, NY

Jane Selden, LaGuardia Community College, NY

Kathy Van Ormer, EDTP UAW-Ford National Programs Center, IL

Rose White, Lindsay Hopkins Technical Education Center, FL

James Wilson, Mount San Antonio College, CA

Finally, I want to thank every student who has ever said to me, "I don't understand." That statement alone has prompted me to try to put into writing answers to important questions. I hope I have succeeded.

—M. E. Sokolik

DEDICATION

★★★

In memory of my grandmother,
Laura Sias

CONTENTS

★★★

V

PREFACE

Rethinking America is a multi-skill cultural series for students of English as a Second Language. Each book has ten broad topic areas. However, the subject matter in these areas varies from book to book. *Rethinking America* incorporates *authentic texts* as a source of reading. Authentic texts give the student an entry into understanding American culture by hearing authentic voices writing about their views and experiences. These readings also represent a variety of genres: newspaper articles and essays, poems, short stories, charts, graphs, and many others.

The readings and activities throughout *Rethinking America* foster cultural awareness, understanding, and interaction among students, and between students and their local setting, whether they are studying English in the U.S. or in another country. This series is intended to get students to examine not only American cultural values, but their own cultural values as well. Through these readings and activities, students engage in meaningful dialogues, and in the process, refine their English language skills.

Many of the changes and additions in this new edition stem from the thoughtful suggestions of students and teachers who have used *Rethinking America* over the years and from the suggestions of reviewers who carefully examined all three new manuscripts as we developed the series. It was extremely gratifying to be able to make use of these ideas as we expanded the original book into a three-book series.

This expansion involved several different types of changes. First of all, there are two new books at the intermediate and high-intermediate levels. Secondly, we have increased the scope of the reading comprehension sections, added specific reading strategies instruction in each chapter, and provided some exciting new ancillary components, including a video segment to accompany each chapter and an Almanac containing supplementary information at the back of each book. Thirdly, all follow-up activities now include exercises which are relevant to students who are using the book in a setting outside of the United States as well as within the U.S.

ORGANIZATION

Chapter Organization Each chapter is organized around a central theme and divided into two subthemes.

Each subtheme contains two readings that examine the topic from different points of view.

INTRODUCTORY MATERIALS

Before You Read Each reading is introduced by a photo, chart, or some other visual opener related to the reading topic. A brief preview of the reading follows, and students are encouraged to think about what they already know about the topic and to answer some questions about the preview.

Cultural Cues Information that may be culture-specific, such as references to television shows or historical figures, is explained before the reading.

About the Author Brief biographies of many of the authors are included. Photos of major figures in American culture are also provided.

THE READING

Each reading includes line numbers for easy reference by the student and teacher. In addition, some words are highlighted for quick reference.

Within each chapter, a video segment related to the topic and obtained from the CNN video archives is listed. Each video clip is accompanied by a set of suggested discussion questions.

EXPANSION MATERIALS

Check Your Comprehension Following each reading are five or more questions regarding the content of the reading.

Reading Strategy A specific reading strategy is highlighted in each follow-up reading activity. A brief statement about the strategy appears in a box in the margin along with a reference to the Reading Strategy Guide in the front of the book which contains a more complete explanation of the strategy.

Vocabulary In this section, students work with the vocabulary from the reading. The activities are varied and designed to keep the interest level high: some ask the students to think about the grammatical context of vocabulary, such as the use of prepositions in idiomatic phrases; some are matching and fill in the blank exercises; still others are games, such as word searches or crossword puzzles.

Think About It This section asks students to go beyond the factual content of a reading and relate their own knowledge and experience to the themes that are introduced. These questions sometimes ask students to apply their understanding to projects, such as participating in simulations, or looking at outside materials such as magazines and newspapers.

Synthesis At the end of each chapter, a section of exercises and activities helps students integrate the ideas presented in the four readings of each chapter. These activities are designed to be relevant to students inside as well as outside the U.S.

Discussion and Debate This section presents several questions that can be used for class discussion or debate. This activity encourages students to come up with their own questions, as well.

Writing Topics The writing topics present different levels of writing tasks, from simple question-and-answer assignments or single-paragraph writing, to journal entries and short essays.

On Your Own This section suggests projects that can be done outside of class. These activities include watching videos, conducting surveys, doing library or Internet research, as well as an array of other student-centered pursuits.

BONUS FEATURES

CNN Video Segments Each volume of the *Rethinking America* series has an accompanying CNN video. The clips on this video are closely tied to one or more of the readings in the *Rethinking America* text. Questions are included in the text to foster discussion of the video. The video transcriptions are available and appear in the Instructor's Manual.

The Almanac An almanac filled with stimulating and rich cultural information is found at the back of each book. It includes a list of major events in U.S. history, maps, temperature conversion tables, and other general information.

Instructor's Manual An Instructor's Manual is available to help make best use of the features of *Rethinking America*. This Manual includes not only answer keys, but also tips for using the video segments, related Internet and other outside information, and guidelines for using the series in EFL settings. The transcriptions for the CNN video also appear in the Instructor's Manual.

Reference Guide to Reading Strategies

★★

Strategies

The following reading strategies are introduced and practiced in *Rethinking America 2*:

Active Reading   Reading actively means creating questions and comments about a text as you read it. This can help you understand and remember ideas and information. As you read, write questions and comments in the margin of your reading.

Finding and Understanding the Main Idea   The main idea is the central, most important idea in the reading. Finding and understanding the main idea will help you understand the central purpose of the reading.

Increasing Speed   By increasing your reading speed, you will actually understand more of what you are reading. When you increase your speed, you read words in groups, rather than individually. This helps you see the connections between the words and phrases in the reading.

Making Predictions   When you make predictions, you use what you already know to make guesses about a reading before beginning the reading. Then, as you read, you check to see if your predictions were accurate. Predictions help you focus and prepare for the reading.

Reading Aloud   Reading Aloud simply means speaking what you are reading, rather than reading silently. When you read aloud you hear the sound of words and phrases. Reading aloud can help you understand new words and information.

Reading Graphics and Statistics   Graphics and statistics allow an author to give a lot of information in a brief and clear way. Graphics and statistics help you to organize information visually and to get a clearer idea of the information appearing in the text.

Scanning   Scanning means reading quickly, without reading every word, in order to *find specific information* in a reading.

Skimming   Skimming means reading quickly, without reading every word, in order to *get the main idea* of a reading. When you skim, look at titles, illustrations and anything else in a reading that will quickly give you information.

Summarizing   Summarizing means taking only the most important ideas and information from a reading and putting them in your own words. Try fitting your summaries on index cards.

Understanding Facts and Opinions   A fact is something that is real and true. An opinion, on the other hand, is what a person believes. An opinion has no proof. t is very important to make sure you understand when what you are reading is fact and when it is opinion.

Understanding Through Outlining   An outline is a numbered, structured grouping of the main points of a reading. Creating an outline helps you understand the structure of a reading by giving you a simplified picture of these main points.

Understanding Arguments   To understand an argument made by an author, you must identify what the author wants to convince you of, and find the ideas the author uses to support this argument.

Understanding by Categorizing   Categorizing means placing information into groups or categories. Putting ideas into two or more different categories can help you get a better understanding of the relationships between ideas in a reading.

Understanding Definitions   Definitions are the meanings of words. Often, the definition of an unfamiliar word can be found in the reading itself. You can learn the meaning of a difficult word by looking at how the word is used in the sentence or surrounding sentences.

Understanding Descriptions   Descriptions are explanations of what something is like. Good descriptions help the reader to get a strong picture of what is being described

---

Understanding Examples   Examples are often used to support main ideas in a reading. Finding these examples will help give you a better understanding of the main points of a reading.

Understanding From Context   Sometimes you can figure out the meaning of a new word or phrase by looking at the other words that come before and after it. These surrounding words can help to show the meaning of the new word or phase.

★★★

CHAPTER 1

The American Dream

What is the American Dream? Is it like other dreams?
In this chapter, you will read about the American Dream
from several different points of view. You will hear from a
modern writer, a poet from the past, the second president of the
United States, and a 20th century president. The American
Dream means something special to each of these people.

PART ONE

Ideas: I HAVE A DREAM

In this section, you will find two very different views of the American Dream. These two selections were written at two different times in America's history, but they share a common theme: hope.

Before You Read

A common view of the American Dream

In this reading, Marilyn vos Savant, a newspaper writer, answers a letter from one of her readers. The reader asks about the meaning of the American Dream.

Before you read these letters, think about these questions:
- Have you heard the phrase "the American Dream" before?
- Do you believe life in the past was easier?
- In your country, were things better in the past?
- How do your parents' lives compare to yours?

Cultural Cues

"During World War II in the foxholes and gun turrets . . ." The writer is speaking of the kinds of dreams that American soldiers had while they were fighting in World War II.

boom box A large portable stereo, known for being loud.

condos Another word for condominiums, types of apartments that are owned, not rented.

Norman Rockwell An American artist (1894–1978) whose works show idealized views of everyday American life.

one side of the ledger An idiom referring to looking at both sides of an issue; a **ledger** is a book for keeping accounts. In a ledger, you write your expenses on one side and your income on the other. If you look at only *one side of the ledger*, you might only look at the negative part of something, for example.

on-line access A connection to the Internet.

white picket fence A small fence, which is a symbol of calm suburban life (see photo).

WHAT IS THE AMERICAN DREAM?

Letter to Marilyn vos Savant

Dear Ms. vos Savant,

You are not a **cynical**[1] person so you may not want to express your opinion about this. What would you say is the "American Dream"? **During World War II, in the foxholes[2] and gun turrets,[3]** the American Dream was a rose-covered cottage with a **white picket fence,** a front porch with

5 a squeaky swing, a shady street, bright and obedient children, camping trips, fishing, the corner soda fountain, and seeing your children taking part in school and church plays. This was depicted by **Norman Rockwell** and early family television shows.

Now we have little **condos, boom boxes** blaring rap and rock, hot rods,

10 drugs, alcohol, cheap sex, abortion, guns, hate and violence. Nearly every sin is applauded on television talk shows. Is there still an "American Dream?

—Robert Kieckhefer, Silver Spring, Maryland

[1]cynical = pessimistic, distrustful

[2]foxhole = a hole dug into the ground to protect a soldier from gunfire

[3]gun turret = a type of tower used to hold guns. Gun turrets are used by the military during battles.

Dear Mr. Kieckhefer,

You're looking at only **one side of the ledger.** First you describe a lovely dream—that few ever really had—and neglect to describe the night-
15 mare aspects of the 1940s (which included some of history's worst moments). You could easily construct a miserable list of social problems **rampant**[4] in the 1950s too. Then you go on to describe only the modern nightmare and imply that modern folks don't have a dream. Of course we do. It's an update on what you already described. I think it would be nice
20 for sweet, old-fashioned folks like you to feel a little better about modern times and become sweet, new-fashioned folks.

Today's "American Dream" includes a house in the suburbs with a back-yard for the kids to play in (instead of a cottage with a fence), a patio for barbecues (instead of a front porch), a shady street, bright and obedient
25 children, camping trips, fishing, two family cars (to take us way past the local ice cream shops), seeing the kids taking part in school and church plays, and **on-line access** to the world. Sounds pretty good to me! The phrasing is a little less romantic and a little more practical, but it's not so different. I only wish we had another Norman Rockwell to celebrate it so
30 well.

Covering one's house with roses is a nice poetic touch if you live in a poetic setting, but in real life I'd vote for growing them in a garden now instead. Which is just what people actually did back in the time period you describe too.

Source: Parade Magazine

Check Your Comprehension

1. Who is Marilyn vos Savant? Who is Mr. Kieckhefer?

2. What does Mr. Kieckhefer think the American Dream is?

3. What does he think of the American Dream today?

4. What does Ms. vos Savant mean when she says, "You're looking at only one side of the ledger?" Which side is Mr. Kieckhefer looking at?

5. What does Ms. vos Savant think of Mr. Kieckhefer's view of the "old" American Dream?

6. Who is Norman Rockwell? Why is he important in these letters?

7. What does the letter writer mean when he says, "You are not a cynical person"?

8. What is Ms. vos Savant's American Dream?

9. What is her opinion of the modern American Dream?

10. Do you think Ms. vos Savant's reply changed Mr. Kieckhefer's opinion? Why or why not?

---

[4]rampant = running wild, overwhelming

 **READING**

Find out more about **understanding arguments** by looking in the Reference Guide to Reading Strategies on pages xii-xiv.

Understanding Arguments

In this reading, the two writers make arguments. That is, each is trying to convince the other of a point of view. What arguments do they make? Use the following table and list the points that each of the writers makes.

Mr. Kieckhefer:	**Ms. vos Savant:**
"The American Dream is dead."	"The American Dream is the same as it was in the past."
_____	_____
_____	_____
_____	_____
_____	_____
_____	_____

Which argument do you agree with? Why?

VOCABULARY
Adjectives

The letter writers include a lot of **adjectives** in their letters. Finish the following sentences showing you understand the meanings of the **boldfaced** words.

1. A **cynical** person would never _____ .

2. A **squeaky** door makes _____ .

3. _____ are very **shady.**

4. An **obedient** child would never _____ .

5. _____ is a **lovely** place.

6. _____ is **rampant** in this country.

7. I think _____ is very **romantic.**

8. _____ is not very **practical.**

9. _____ sounds very **poetic.**

10. A **bright** student _____ .

THINK ABOUT IT

1. How "American" is the American Dream? Do people of other countries have similar dreams? How is the American Dream different?

2. There is a popular saying in the United States: "A pessimist sees the glass as half-empty, the optimist sees it as half-full." Mr. Kieckhefer

seems to be a pessimist, and Ms. vos Savant an optimist. Which are you? Why do you think so?

3. What is your dream? Is it similar to the American Dream? How is it different?

Before You Read

The Life of Walt Whitman

1819	born May 31, the second of nine children in West Hills, Long Island, New York to Walter and Louisa Whitman
1823	the Whitman family moved to Brooklyn, New York
1825–30	Whitman's only years of formal education
1831	Whitman worked as a clerk in a law office
1835	began work as a printer
1836	began working as a teacher
1838	became editor of the *Long Islander*, a weekly newspaper
1840	worked for the Presidential campaign of Martin van Buren
1841	left teaching and became a printer for the *New World* and a reporter for the *Democratic Review*
1842	published his first and only novel, *Franklin Evans*
1842–44	edited the *Aurora*, a daily newspaper, and the *Evening Tattler*
1845–48	returned to Brooklyn to write for and edit several newspapers
1848	worked briefly for the *Crescent*, New Orleans
1848–49	edited *The Brooklyn Freeman*
1850–54	ran a stationery store, a printing office, and built houses
1855	published *Leaves of Grass*, a volume of poetry, at his own expense
1857–59	edited *The Brooklyn Times*
1861–64	volunteered in hospitals during the Civil War
1873	suffered a stroke
1892	died in Camden, New Jersey

The following poem was written by Walt Whitman, who is known as one of America's greatest poets.

Before you read this poem, think about the following questions:

• Do you enjoy poetry?

• What poets do you enjoy reading in English or in your native language?

Cultural Cues   *ploughboy* A young man who works on a farm with a "plough," or "plow," as it is spelled today.

I Hear America Singing
by Walt Whitman

I hear America singing, the varied **carols**[1] I hear,
Those of mechanics, each one singing his as it should be **blithe**[2] and
    strong,
The carpenter singing his as he measures his **plank or beam**[3],
5 The **mason**[4] singing his as he makes ready for work, or leaves off work,
The boatman singing what belongs to him in his boat, the **deck-hand**[5]
    singing on the steamboat deck.
The shoemaker singing as he sits on his bench, the hatter singing as he
    stands,
10 The wood-cutter's song, the **ploughboy's** on his way in the morning, or
    at noon intermission or at sundown,
The delicious singing of the mother, or of the young wife at work, or of
    the girl sewing or washing,
Each singing what belongs to him or her and to none else,
15 The day what belongs to the day—at night the party of young fellows,
    robust[6], friendly,
Singing with open mouths their strong melodious songs.

Source: *Leaves of Grass*

Check Your Comprehension

1. Who are the characters in this poem?

2. Why do you think the characters are singing?

3. What does the line, "each one singing his as it should be blithe and strong" mean?

4. What does the line, "Each singing what belongs to him or her and to none else" mean?

[1]carol = song
[2]blithe = cheerful
[3]plank or beam = types of wood
[4]mason = brick worker
[5]deck-hand = someone who works on a boat (on the deck)
[6]robust = healthy

5. What does "the day what belongs to the day" mean?

6. What is the mood (happy, sad, thoughtful, etc.) of this poem?

7. What is the main idea of this poem?

8. What is Whitman's view of the American Dream?

READING

Find out more about **reading aloud** by looking in the Reference Guide to Reading Strategies on pages xii-xiv.

Reading Aloud

Poems are often understood better when read aloud. You get a stronger sense of the rhythm, rhyme, and sound of the words, all which add to the meaning. Practice reading the poem aloud. If you are good at memorizing things, try memorizing the poem and reciting it.

VOCABULARY
Professions

This crossword puzzle uses the names of professions found in this poem. Read the descriptions of the professions, and write the correct words in the blanks.

Across

1. Someone who works on a ship
4. Someone who makes boots and sandals
7. Someone who works the soil on a farm
9. Someone who makes hats
10. Someone who builds furniture

Down

2. A woman with children
3. Someone who chops trees for fires
5. Someone who works on engines
6. Someone who works on the deck of a boat
8. Someone who builds with stone or brick

THINK ABOUT IT

1. Whitman is famous for his poem in honor of Abraham Lincoln, "O Captain, My Captain." Find it on the Internet or in the library and bring it to class for discussion.

2. "I Hear America Singing" is called a lyric poem, that is, a poem that brings forth certain feelings or emotions. What emotions do you think Whitman was trying to bring forth in his readers?

3. This poem shows a difference between men and women. How does it do that? Why do you think this difference exists?

PART TWO

OUR LEADERS: The Pursuit of Happiness

These two readings are from opposite ends of the history of the United States. The Declaration of Independence is one of the first important documents created by the new American government. President Clinton's speech is quite recent.

Before You Read

The Declaration of Independence

The next reading is the text of the Declaration of Independence, signed on July 4, 1776. In it, the leaders of America declared that America should be free from England.

The language of this reading is from a different time period, and therefore isn't like modern English. You will see two versions here: one in the original language, and one in modern English. Read it first in the original, as the language is an important part of American culture. Then, read the modern version to deepen your understanding.

 Watch the CNN video on Independence Day.

Discuss these questions:

1. How is Independence Day celebrated across the United States?

2. What activity do most Americans take part in on Independence Day?

Before you read, think about the following questions:

• Did your country ever go through a revolutionary war?

• What do you know about the American Revolution?

Declaration of Independence
In Congress, July 4, 1776

The unanimous Declaration of the thirteen united States of America,

When in the Course of human events, it becomes necessary for one people to dissolve the political bands which have connected them with another, and to assume among the powers of the earth, the separate and
5 equal station to which the Laws of Nature and of Nature's God entitle them, a decent respect to the opinions of mankind requires that they should declare the causes which impel them to the separation.

We hold these truths to be self-evident, that all men are created equal, that they are endowed by their Creator with certain unalienable Rights, that
10 among these are Life, Liberty and the Pursuit of Happiness.—That to secure these rights, Governments are instituted among Men, deriving their just powers from the consent of the governed, —That whenever any Form of Government becomes destructive of these ends, it is the Right of the People to alter or to abolish it, and to institute new Government, laying its founda-
15 tion on such principles and organizing its powers in such form, as to them shall seem most likely to effect their Safety and Happiness. Prudence, indeed, will dictate that Governments long established should not be changed for light and transient causes; and accordingly all experience **hath shewn**[1], that mankind are more disposed to suffer, while evils are sufferable, than
20 to right themselves by abolishing the forms to which they are accustomed.

In "plain English":

The declaration of all thirteen united States of America.

In history, when one group of people needs to declare itself free from another, and to become free as God and Nature intends them to be, it is
25 necessary that they explain why they are declaring their freedom.

We believe our reasons are obvious, that all men are created equal, that God has given them certain rights which cannot be violated, including, life, liberty, and the pursuit of happiness. Governments are formed to protect these rights, and governments get their power from the people. Whenever
30 one government works against human rights, the people have the right to end that government and start a new one which will bring about safety and happiness. Of course, cautious people know that old governments should not be changed for minor reasons; furthermore, experience has shown that people are more willing to suffer things that are not horrible than to get rid
35 of governments that they are used to.

[1]hath shewn = has shown

Check Your Comprehension

1. According to the Declaration, when should people form new governments?

2. According to the Declaration, when should people not form new governments?

3. What are the basic human rights, according to the Declaration?

4. What does "the separate and equal station" mean?

5. What does "that mankind are more disposed to suffer, while evils are sufferable, than to right themselves by abolishing the forms to which they are accustomed" mean?

6. What does "deriving their just powers from the consent of the governed" mean?

 READING

Find out more about **summarizing** by looking in the Reference Guide to Reading Strategies on pages xii–xiv.

Summarizing

The plain English version of the Declaration is a type of summary. Write another summary, even shorter than the simplified version.

_____

_____

_____

_____

_____

Compare your version with one written by another student in the class. What information did you include that your partner did not? Do you want to rewrite your summary after reading your partner's?

VOCABULARY
Using New Words

Choose the best synonym for each of these words.

1. *dissolve*
   a. discontinue
   b. fix
   c. dislocate
   d. unite

2. *entitle*
   a. name
   b. authorize
   c. prevent
   d. belittle

3. *evident*
   a. right
   b. clear
   c. untrue
   d. helpful

4. *consent*
   a. permission
   b. continuous
   c. expense
   d. denial

5. *destructive*
   a. supportive
   b. noisy
   c. harmful
   d. creative

6. *institute*
   a. deserve
   b. begin
   c. end
   d. want

7. *dictate*
   a. say
   b. want
   c. give
   d. harm

8. *transient*
   a. important
   b. moving
   c. unimportant
   d. temporary

9. *abolish*
   a. end
   b. begin
   c. keep
   d. want

10. *suffer*
    a. harm
    b. endure
    c. keep
    d. begin

THINK ABOUT IT

1. At one time, Great Britain had many colonies, including the United States. Do you know what some of the others were? What colonies does Great Britain still rule?

2. What does independence mean to you? Are you independent? Why is it such an important value, in your opinion?

3. In your opinion, when is revolution necessary? Would you participate in a revolution? Under what circumstances?

Before You Read

The Life of President Bill Clinton

William Jefferson Clinton
42nd President of the United States, (beginning on January 20, 1993)

Nickname: Bill

Born: August 19, 1946, in Hope, Arkansas

Father: William Jefferson Blythe III

Stepfather: Roger Clinton

Mother: Virginia Divine Blythe Clinton

Married: Hillary Rodham, on October 11, 1975

Children: Chelsea Victoria Clinton

Religion: Baptist

Education: Graduated from Georgetown University (1968); attended Oxford University (1968–70); graduated from Yale University Law School (1973)

Occupation: Lawyer, public official

Political Party: Democrat

Other Government Positions:

- Arkansas Attorney General, 1976–78

- Governor of Arkansas, 1978–80, 1982–92

READING

Finding out more about **making predictions** by looking in the Reference Guide to Reading Strategies on pages xii–xiv.

Making Predictions

The next reading consists of part of the January 1997 inaugural speech given by President Clinton. Inaugural speeches are ones given on the day that the President takes office after being elected.

You probably already know something about political speeches. Think about the political speeches you have heard, either in English or in another language, and see what **predictions** you can make about the reading. Do this *before* you read. First think about the **purpose** of an inaugural speech. Discuss this with your class.

What topics do you think this speech will cover? Check the boxes. After you finish reading, return to this chart and decide whether your predictions were correct.

Topic	After reading: Were you right?
☐ taxes	
☐ housing	
☐ unemployment	
☐ health care	
☐ education	
☐ religion	
☐ crime	
☐ democracy	
☐ freedom	
☐ international trade	
☐ the opposing party	
☐ the Internet	
☐ foreign relations	

Cultural Cues   *Industrial Revolution* A period on change in the late eighteenth century in England, when factories were becoming mechanized. The Industrial Revolution caused many changes not only in the workplace, but in society and culture as well.

About the Author   William J. Clinton is the 42nd President of the United States. Born in Hope, Arkansas, Mr. Clinton attended Yale University and Oxford University. He became President for the first time in 1993, and was the first President from the Democratic Party in twelve years. He was elected a second time in 1996, during a prosperous period in the American economy.

Second Inaugural Address of
President William J. Clinton

January 20, 1997

My fellow citizens:

At this last presidential inauguration of the twentieth century, let us lift our eyes toward the challenges that await us in the next century. It is our
5 great good fortune that time and chance have put us not only at the edge of a new century, in a new **millennium**[1], but on the edge of a bright new prospect in human affairs—a moment that will define our course, and our character, for decades to come. We must keep our old democracy forever young. Guided by the ancient vision of a promised land, let us set our sights
10 upon a land of new promise.

The promise of America was born in the eighteenth century out of the bold conviction that we are all created equal. It was extended and preserved

[1]millennium = 1,000 years

in the nineteenth century, when our nation spread across the continent, saved the union, and **abolished**[2] the awful **scourge**[3] of slavery.

15 Then, in **turmoil**[4] and triumph, that promise exploded onto the world stage to make this the American Century.

And what a century it has been. America became the world's mightiest industrial power; saved the world from **tyranny**[5] in two world wars and a long cold war; and time and again, reached out across the globe to millions
20 who, like us, longed for the blessings of liberty.

Along the way, Americans produced a great middle class and security in old age; built unrivaled centers of learning and opened public schools to all; split the atom and explored the heavens; invented the computer and the microchip; and deepened the **wellspring**[6] of justice by making a revolution
25 in civil rights for African-Americans and all minorities, and extending the circle of citizenship, opportunity and dignity to women.

Now, for the third time, a new century is upon us, and another time to choose. We began the nineteenth century with a choice, to spread our nation from coast to coast. We began the twentieth century with a choice, to
30 harness the **Industrial Revolution** to our values of free enterprise, conservation, and human decency. Those choices made all the difference. At the dawn of the twenty-first century a free people must now choose to shape the forces of the Information Age and the global society, to unleash the limitless potential of all our people, and, yes, to form a more perfect union.

35 When last we gathered, our march to this new future seemed less certain than it does today. We vowed then to set a clear course to renew our nation.

In these four years, we have been touched by tragedy, exhilarated by challenge, strengthened by achievement. America stands alone as the world's indispensable nation. Once again, our economy is the strongest on Earth.
40 Once again, we are building stronger families, thriving communities, better educational opportunities, a cleaner environment. Problems that once seemed destined to deepen now bend to our efforts: our streets are safer and record numbers of our fellow citizens have moved from welfare to work.

45 And once again, we have resolved for our time a great debate over the role of government. Today we can declare: Government is not the problem, and government is not the solution. We—the American people—we are the solution. Our founders understood that well and gave us a democracy strong enough to endure for centuries, flexible enough to face our common chal-
50 lenges and advance our common dreams in each new day.

---

[2]abolished = ended

[3]scourge = illness, affliction

[4]turmoil = an unsettled condition

[5]tyranny = oppression, dictatorship

[6]wellspring = source, fountain

Check Your Comprehension

1. What is unique about President Clinton's 1997 inauguration?

2. President Clinton says, "The promise of America was born in the eighteenth century out of the bold conviction that we are all created equal." What is he referring to?

3. What events took place in America in the nineteenth century, according to the President?

4. Why does the President call the twentieth century "the American Century"?

5. What does the phrase, "problems that once seemed destined to deepen now bend to our efforts" mean? What problems does he mean?

6. What will be the challenge of the twenty-first century, according to the President?

7. What do you think this sentence means: "Today we can declare: Government is not the problem, and government is not the solution"?

8. What are the successes of the President's first four years in office, according to the speech?

VOCABULARY
Adjectives
-ed and *-ing* endings

This reading contains some adjectives, words that describe nouns, that end in *-ed* and *-ing*. It also contains some verbs that end in *-ed* and *-ing*. How can you tell when one of these words is being used as an adjective and when it is being used as a verb? When the *-ed* and *-ing* word comes before a noun and describes that noun, it is being used as an adjective. When the word is part of a verb phrase, it is being used as a verb.

Here are two examples:

I was <u>surprised</u> by the news.

That is very <u>surprising</u> news.

In the first example, "surprised" is part of the verb phrase "was surprised." In the second example, "surprising" comes before the noun "news" and describes the news—surprising news.

Look at the underlined words from the reading and write **A** if the word is being used as an adjective and **V** if it is being used as a verb.

<u>A</u> 1. America is the <u>promised</u> land.

_____ 2. We are all <u>created</u> equal.

_____ 3. We have built <u>unrivaled</u> centers of learning.

_____ 4. We have <u>explored</u> the heavens.

_____ 5. We are <u>extending</u> the rights of citizenship to all.

_____ 6. We are building <u>thriving</u> communities.

THINK ABOUT IT

1. What is your opinion of this inaugural speech? Did you learn anything from it?

2. What connections do you find between this speech and the Declaration of Independence? Why do you think those connections exist?

3. In your library, or on the Internet, locate a recording of a political speech and listen to it. Write your impressions in your journal. Discuss the speech with your class.

SYNTHESIS

Discussion and Debate

1. Each of the four readings in this chapter present a view of America. Describe the four views. How are they similar? How do they differ?

2. These four readings look at America at different points in time: 1776, 1855, and the mid-1990s. What differences are there in the readings that are related to the historical events?

3. All of the readings in this chapter present an optimistic, or positive, view of America. What is left out? Do you think there is another part of the story that isn't being told? Is that part less important?

4. Ask your classmates another question about this chapter.

Writing Topics

1. Look at the timeline of Walt Whitman's life presented in this chapter. Using that information, write a short essay about his life.

2. Write a new version of "I Hear America Singing". Make it relevant to modern life. You may write an essay, or a poem, if you prefer.

3. Write an essay in which you explain what the American Dream means in today's world. You can write about what the Dream means to you personally, or to people in general.

On Your Own

1. Identify a period of American history that interests you. Do a little research on the Internet or in the library and find out more about that period. Give a short presentation to your class about your research.

2. The following films deal with America's history or government. Choose one of them to watch—check it out of the library or rent it from a video store.

All the President's Men	*Glory*
Being There	*Mr. Smith Goes to Washington*
Bob Roberts	*The American President*
Gettysburg	*The Candidate*
Wag the Dog	*Primary Colors*

3. Find a Presidential speech on the Internet
    (http://www.whitehouse.gov). Read it.

4. How much do people know about American history? Interview at
    least three people and ask them the following questions. (If you are in
    the United States, try to ask Americans.) Compare your responses
    with your classmates' responses.

    a. When was the country established?

    b. Who was its first leader?

    c. When was the first World War?

    Add other questions that you think might be interesting (don't make
    them too hard!). Compare your answers with your classmates'
    answers. What conclusions can you draw?

★★

A L M A N A C   For additional cultural information, refer to the Almanac on pages 217–228.
The Almanac contains lists of useful facts, maps, and other information to
enhance your learning.

★★★

CHAPTER 2

Money

America is often thought of as a wealthy country. Its citizens are known for working long hours with little vacation time. However, they are also known for enjoying the money they earn. In this chapter, you will read about American working habits and American attitudes towards money.

PART ONE

The Economy
Working to Live—Living to Work

Do you enjoy working? In this section, two very different Americans talk
about their homes and work,
and how these two areas of life relate to each other.

Before You Read

In this reading, the author talks to a woman about her work and her family.
You may be surprised to read about the woman's attitude towards her work
at a factory.

Before you read, think about the following questions:

- What kinds of jobs have you had? Did you enjoy working?
- Do you enjoy spending time with your family?
- Do people spend enough time with their families?

Cultural Cues

Walgreens A large chain of drugstores that is part of the Sam Walton
family businesses, which also includes Wal-Mart; the Waltons are among
the three richest families in the United States.

Men and Women in the Workforce

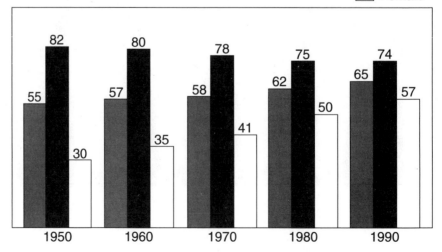

Percent in Labor Force
by Sex: 1950 to 1990

Legend: Total (dark gray), Male (black), Female (white)

Year	Total	Male	Female
1950	55	82	30
1960	57	80	35
1970	58	78	41
1980	62	75	50
1990	65	74	57

Source: "Labor Force and
Occupation," Peter J. Sepielli
and Thomas J. Palumbo,
Friday, May 9, 1997, U.S.
Census Bureau, http://
www.census.gov/population/
www/pop-profile/lfoccu.html

READING

Find out more about **reading graphics and statistics** by looking in the Reference Guide to Reading Strategies on pages xii–xiv.

Reading Graphics and Statistics

The graph above shows statistics about men and women in the work force. Look closely at the graph, which reports percentages, and answer the following questions:

1. Between 1950 and 1990, the percentage of all people working _____ .

   a. grew   **b.** fell   **c.** stayed about the same

2. The percentage of women in the workforce grew the most between

   _____ .

   a. 1950–1960   **b.** 1960–1970
   c. 1970–1980   **d.** 1980–1990

3. The percentage of men employed dropped 3 percent between _____ .

   a. 1950–1960   **b.** 1960–1970
   c. 1970–1980   **d.** 1980–1990

4. There is a 17% difference between the number of men and women in

   the workforce in _____ .

   a. 1960   **b.** 1970
   c. 1980   **d.** 1990

5. What do you predict the percentages will be for the year 2000,

   based on this chart? _____

   a. 68, 72, 66   **b.** 56, 72, 59   **c.** 80, 88, 78

Explain your answer.

About the Author   Arlie Hochschild is a professor of Sociology at the University of California, Berkeley. She is the author of two popular books on American life: *The Second Shift* and *The Managed Heart*. Her work has also appeared in many magazines, including *Psychology Today* and *Harper's*. She has received many awards for her work.

Family Values and Reversed Worlds
by Arlie Russell Hochschild

Linda Avery* a friendly thirty-eight-year-old mother of two daughters, is a shift supervisor at the Demco Plant, ten miles down the valley from Amerco headquarters. Her husband, Bill, is a technician in the same plant. Linda and Bill share the care of her sixteen-year-old daughter from a previous

5   marriage and their two-year-old by working opposite shifts, as a full fifth of American working parents do. "Bill works the 7 A.M. to 3 P.M. shift while I watch the baby," Linda explained. "Then I work the 3 P.M. to 11 P.M. shift and he watches the baby. My older daughter works at **Walgreens** after school."

10   When we first met in the factory's breakroom over a couple of Cokes, Linda was in blue jeans and a pink jersey, her hair pulled back in a long ponytail. She wore no makeup, and her manner was purposeful and direct. She was working overtime, and so I began by asking her whether Amerco required the overtime, or whether she volunteered for it. "Oh, I put in for

15   it," she replied with a low chuckle. But, I wondered aloud, wouldn't she and her husband like to have more time at home together, finances and company policy permitting. Linda took off her safety glasses, rubbed her whole face, folded her arms, resting her elbows on the table, and approached the question by describing her life at home:

20   I walk in the door and the minute I turn the key in the lock my older daughter is there. Granted, she needs somebody to talk to about her day. . . . The baby is still up. She should have been in bed two hours ago and that upsets me. The dishes are piled in the sink. My daughter comes right up to the door and complains about anything her stepfather

25   said or did, and she wants to talk about her job. My husband is in the other room hollering to my daughter, "Tracy, I don't *ever* get any time to talk to your mother, because you're always monopolizing her time before I even get a chance!" They all come at me at once.

30   To Linda, her home was not a place to relax. It was another workplace. Her description of the urgency of demands and the **unarbitrated**[1] quarrels that awaited her homecoming contrasted with her account of arriving at her job as a shift supervisor:

      I usually come to work early just to get away from the house. I get

35   there at 2:30 P.M., and people are there waiting. We sit. We talk. We joke.

---

*The names of the people and the company name in this reading have been changed.

[1]unarbitrated = not worked out, not controlled

I let them know what's going on, who has to be where, what changes I've made for the shift that day. We sit and chit-chat for five or ten minutes. There's laughing, joking, fun. My coworkers aren't putting me down for any reason. Everything is done with humor and fun from
40 beginning to end, though it can get stressful when a machine malfunctions.

For Linda, home had become work and work had become home. Somehow, the two worlds had been reversed. Indeed, Linda felt she could only get relief from the "work" of being at home by going to the "home" of work.
45 . . . In a previous era, men regularly escaped the house for the bar, the fishing hole, the golf course, the pool hall, or often enough, the sweet joy of work. Today, as one of the women who make up 45 percent of the American workforce, Linda Avery, overloaded and feeling unfairly treated at home, was escaping to work, too. Nowadays, men and women both may
50 leave unwashed dishes, unresolved quarrels, crying tots, testy teenagers, and unresponsive mates behind to arrive at work early and call out, "Hi, fellas, I'm here!"
. . . Where did Linda feel most relaxed? She laughed more, joked more, listened to more interesting stories while on break at the factory than at
55 home. The social life that once might have surrounded her at home she now found at work. Frankly, life there was more fun.

Source: *The Time Bind*

Check Your Comprehension

1. What does Linda mean when she says she "put in for" overtime?

2. According to the reading, how many parents work at opposite times?

3. How have working women become like working men, according to this reading?

4. At the time the author wrote this article, what percentage of women were in the workforce?

5. Why does Linda prefer work to home?

6. In the past, where did men go to escape the pressures of home?

7. What do you think is the meaning of "reversed worlds" in the title?

8. Why is work more fun than home to some Americans, according to the reading?

VOCABULARY
Understanding Idioms and Colloquial Language

This reading contains idioms and colloquial language. These items are in *italics* in the sentences below. Choose the sentence that is closest in meaning to the original sentence. Explain your answer.

1. We *chit-chat* for five or ten minutes.
   a. We speak seriously for five or ten minutes.
   b. We speak lightly for five or ten minutes.
   c. We speak angrily for five or ten minutes.

2. Her daughter was a *testy* teenager.
   a. Her daughter was a happy teenager.
   b. Her daughter was a smart teenager.
   c. Her daughter was a short-tempered teenager.

3. Her coworkers didn't *put her down*.
   a. Her coworkers didn't criticize her.
   b. Her coworkers didn't leave her alone.
   c. Her coworkers didn't work with her.

4. My husband *hollered to* my daughter.
   a. My husband scolded my daughter.
   b. My husband yelled to my daughter.
   c. My husband laughed at my daughter.

5. She went to her favorite *fishing hole*.
   a. She went to her favorite lake.
   b. She went to her favorite fish market.
   c. She went to her favorite restaurant.

THINK ABOUT IT

1. What is life like for working parents in your culture?

2. In what ways is your family like the Avery family in the reading? In what ways is your family different?

3. Do you think Linda Avery is a bad mother? Why or why not?

4. What advice would you give the Avery family for improving their relationships? Write a letter to them giving them your advice.

Before You Read

Housing and Unemployment

City	Percent Unemployed	Average House Price
Austin, Texas	3.3	$111,800
Minneapolis, Minnesota	3.4	111,500
Phoenix, Arizona	3.8	102,600
Honolulu, Hawaii	4.6	331,800
Denver, Colorado	4.8	130,500
Las Vegas, Nevada	5.3	117,600
Boston, Massachusetts	5.4	187,300
Dallas, Texas	5.9	100,800
Seattle, Washington	6.1	160,700
San Francisco, California	6.1	252,200
San Diego, California	6.5	173,800
Chicago, Illinois	6.7	149,800
Atlanta, Georgia	7.3	98,500
Philadelphia, Pennsylvania	7.6	118,700
New York City, New York	8.2	169,000
Baltimore, Maryland	8.3	109,700
Los Angeles, California	8.9	172,100
Miami, Florida	10.5	109,800

Look carefully at the table and answer these questions:

- Which city do you think is the easiest city for a low-income family to move to?
- Which city would be the most difficult to move to?
- Which city would you like to move to?

Explain your answers.

READING

Find out more about **skimming** by looking in the Reference Guide to Reading Strategies on pages xii–xiv.

Skimming

Skimming means reading something quickly to get the main idea. Skim the article "Homeless" from *Rachel and Her Children*. Take no more than three minutes. Here are some hints on how to skim:

- Move your eyes quickly down the page. Don't stop on individual words.

- Slow down a little when you see something that looks important to you.
- Put a check in the margin, or underline important phrases—but don't do this often. Remember, keep moving!

Now answer the questions below.

1. What is the main point of this story? _____

_____

2. Who is Richard Lazarus? _____

_____

3. How did Mr. Lazarus become homeless? _____

_____

Finally, read the story as you normally would.

In the following reading, the author went into the subway in New York and found a homeless man to talk to. Here, he tells a little about what it is like to be homeless.

Before you read, think about the following questions:
- Who is responsible for the homeless?
- Are there homeless people in your city? How do you feel about them?
- Do you think homeless people are lazy?

Cultural Cues

The Bowery An area of New York City, now well known for the number of homeless people and transients who stay there.

Dante An Italian poet (1265–1321) who wrote *The Divine Comedy*, one part of which, "The Inferno," gives a detailed description of Hell.

Grand Central Station One of the major railroad and subway stations in New York City.

Grand Hyatt A large hotel in New York City.

Macy's A large department store.

Martinique The name of a hotel used as a shelter for the homeless in New York City.

Medicaid A government healthcare program primarily for poor and elderly people.

Port Authority A public transportation station in New York City.

Vietnam veteran Someone who was part of the military during the Vietnam War.

About the Author   Jonathan Kozol is the author of the National Book Award-winning *Death at an Early Age,* as well as many other books, including *Savage Inequalities: Children in America's Schools, Amazing Grace: The Lives of Children and the Conscience of a Nation,* and *Illiterate America.* Over the past 30 years he has been concerned with the care and education of children.

"Homeless" from Rachel and Her Children

by Jonathan Kozol

Richard Lazarus, an educated, 36–year-old **Vietnam veteran** I met two days after Thanksgiving in the subway underneath **Grand Central Station**, tells me he had never been
5 without a job until the recent summer. In July he underwent the loss of job, children, and wife, all in a single stroke. As in almost all these situations, it was the simultaneous occurrence of a number of emergencies, any one of
10 which he might have sustained alone, but not all at the same time, that suddenly removed him from his home.

"Always, up until last summer, I have found a job that paid at least $300. Now I couldn't
15 find a job that paid $200. When I found an opening at a department store they said that I was overqualified. If someone had asked me a year ago who are the homeless, I would not have known what to reply. Now I know
20 the answer. They are people like myself. I went to Catholic elementary school. I had my secondary education in a private military school. I joined the service and was sent to Thailand as an airman." He has a trade. It's
25 known as "inventory data processing." He had held a single job in data processing for seven years until last summer when the company shut down, without a warning, and moved out of state.
30 "When the company left I could find nothing. I looked everywhere. I got one job for two months in the summer. Part-time, as a security

guard in one of the hotels for homeless families."

35 When I ask which one it was, he says the **Martinique**. "I clocked the floors for fire check. From the top floor to the lobby I swore to myself: rat infested, roach infested, drug in-

fested, filth infested, garbage everywhere, and little children playing in the stairs. Innocent people, women, children, boxed in by their misery. Most people are permitted to make more than one mistake. Not when you're poor."

In September he was sick. "I was guarding homeless people and I didn't have a home. I slept in Washington Square and Central Park." He's living now in a run-down hotel operated in conjunction with the Third Street Shelter on **the Bowery**. "When you come in at night the guards wear gloves. They check you with a metal detector. They're afraid to touch me."

While we talk we watch an old man nearby who is standing flat and motionless against the wall, surrounded by two dozen bright-red shopping bags from **Macy's**. Every so often, someone stops to put a coin into his hand. I notice the care with which the people drop their coins, in order that their hands do not touch his. When I pass that spot some hours later, he will still be there. I'll do the same. I'll look at his hand—the fingers worn and swollen and the nails curled in like claws—and I will drop a quarter and extract my hand and move off quickly.

After standing with Lazarus for two hours before the hot-dog stand, I ask him if he'd like to leave the station to sit down with me and get a decent meal. He's awkward about accepting this. When I press him, he explains he had only one subway **token**[1] and has no more money. If he leaves the station he will need a dollar to get back inside. He agrees to leave when I assure him I can spare a dollar. Outside on Forty-Second Street, we're facing the **Grand Hyatt**. He looks at it with fear.

"The first thing that you see when you come out of there is power."

At a delicatessen next to the Grand Hyatt he explains about the subway tokens. Each morning at the shelter you get in a line in order to receive two subway tokens. This is to enable you to look for jobs; the job search is required. But, in order to get the tokens, you have got to prove that you already have a job appointment. "It's a long line. By the time you get the tokens you have missed the job appointment. You wait in line for everything. I get the feeling that the point is not to find a job but to teach us something about who we are. Getting us in line is the idea."

In the restaurant he orders a chicken sandwich and, although he's nervous and his hands are shaking, he eats fast; he's almost done before I've put a paper napkin in my lap. He apologizes but he tells me that this is the first thing he has had to eat since 8:00 A.M. It's now about 8:30 in the evening.

"Before I got into this place I was sleeping in the parks. When it got colder I would sleep all night in an X-rated movie or the subway or the **Port Authority**. I'd spend most of my time just walking. I would try to bathe each day in public toilets. I'd wash my clothes and lay them outside in the sun to dry. I didn't want to feel like a **pariah**[2] that nobody would get near. I used to talk with people like yourself so that I would not begin to feel cut off. I invested all my strength in fighting off depression. I was scared that I would fall apart.

"During this time I tried to reunite with my old lady. For me, the loss of work and loss of wife had left me rocking. Then the welfare regulations hit me. I began to feel that I would be reduced to trash. You're never prepared for this. It's like there isn't any bottom. It's not like cracks in a safety net. It's like a black hole sucking you inside. Half the people that I know are suffering from chest infections and sleep deprivation. The lack of sleep leaves you **debilitated,**[3] shaky. You exaggerate your fears. If a psychiatrist came along he'd say that I was crazy. But I was an ordinary man. There was nothing wrong with me. I lost my wife. I lost my kids. I lost my home. Now would you say that I was crazy if I told you I was feeling sad?

"I was a pretty stable man. Now I tremble

[1]token = coin used for subway entry

[2]pariah = social outcast

[3]debilitated = sick, unable to function

when I meet somebody in the ordinary world. I'm trembling right now. One reason that I didn't want to leave the subway was that I feel safer underground. When you asked if I would come
130 outside and get something to eat, my first thought was that you would see me shaking if we sat down for a meal and you'd think I was an alcoholic.

"I've had a bad cold for two weeks. When
135 you're sick there's no way to get better. You cannot sleep in at the shelter. You have got to go outside and show that you are looking for a job. I had **asthma**[4] as a kid. It was gone for twenty years. Now it's back. I'm always
140 swallowing for air. Before I got into the shelter, I did not have **Medicaid** or welfare. If you don't have an address it's very hard. I scrambled to get into the computer.

"Asthma's common at the shelter. There's a
145 lot of dust. That may be why. Edema [swollen feet]—you get it from sitting up so much and walking all day long. If you're very hungry and you want a meal you can get it at St. Francis. You can get a sandwich at Grand Central every
150 night at ten o'clock. So if you want to keep from starving you are always on the move. If you have no subway tokens then you jump the stile. You're always breaking rules and so you start to have this sense of **premonition**[5]:

[4]asthma = a type of illness that makes it difficult to breathe
[5]premonition = a feeling about the future

155 'Sooner or later I'll be caught.' You live in constant fear.

"A year ago I never thought that somebody like me would end up in a shelter. Nothing you've ever undergone prepares you. You walk
160 into the place—the smell of sweat and urine hits you like a wall. Unwashed bodies and the look of absolute despair on many, many faces there would make you think you were in **Dante**'s Hell. Abandon hope. I read a lot. I'm
165 not a lazy man.

"I slept with my clothes on the first night that I was there. I was given a cot but they were out of sheets. I lay awake. I heard men crying in their sleep. They're sound asleep and
170 they are crying. What you fear is that you will be here forever. You do not know if it's ever going to end. You think to yourself: It is a dream and I will wake. Sometimes I think: It's an experiment. They are watching you to find out
175 how much you can take. Someone will come someday and say: 'Okay, this guy has suffered long enough. Now we'll take him back into our world.' Then you wake up and get in line. . . .

"Listen to me: I've always worked. I need
180 to work! I'm not a lazy man." His voice rises and the people at the other tables stare. "If I thought that I could never work again I'd want to die."

Source: *Rachel and Her Children*

Check Your Comprehension

1. What is Richard Lazarus's background? What is his occupation?
2. Why is Mr. Lazarus homeless?
3. What is the irony about Mr. Lazarus working at the Martinique Hotel?
4. Mr. Lazarus gives two reasons why he doesn't like to come out of the subway. What are they?
5. Why is Mr. Lazarus surprised that he has become homeless?
6. What is wrong with homeless shelters, according to Mr. Lazarus?
7. Mr. Lazarus says that he thinks it might be "an experiment." What does he mean?
8. Richard Lazarus says, "Getting us in line is the idea." What does he mean by this?
9. According to the reading, what type of person can become homeless?

VOCABULARY
Using Prepositions

Write the correct preposition(s) on the line(s) in each of the following sentences.

1. The benefit dinner was given _____ conjunction

_____ a charity auction.

2. You should try to find _____ how to help the homeless.

3. No one enjoys waiting _____ line.

4. If you stay _____ your room alone, you might begin to feel

cut _____ from society.

5. I was invited _____ two dinner parties, but they were

both _____ the same time.

6. I went to visit my old friend, but his landlord said he had moved

_____ .

7. His room was so small, he felt boxed _____ .

8. Donna went _____ bed very late last night, so she is

sleeping _____ this morning.

9. Most people don't believe they will ever end _____ homeless.

10. The desk was surrounded _____ a lot of empty boxes.

THINK ABOUT IT

1. According to the article, Mr. Lazarus is educated, has at least seven years of experience in his trade, and wants to work.
Why do you think he doesn't have a job?

2. Mr. Lazarus says he never thought he could become homeless. Do you think you could ever be homeless? Why or why not?

3. What would you do if you were Mr. Lazarus?

4. How did this reading make you feel? Were you surprised by anything? Did anything make you sad? Angry? Explain your answer.

5. Imagine Mr. Lazarus two years from now. Write a description of what happens to him beginning after the author of the reading interviewed him.

PART TWO

MONEY MAKES THE WORLD GO AROUND

How much money do you spend? How much do you save? In this section, you will read about American attitudes towards saving and spending money.

Before You Read

Gather different denominations of American money, if you can. Look at the pictures on the money, and read the following table.

Most Common Denominations of U.S. Currency

Amount	Portrait	Design on the Back
$1	George Washington	The great seal of the United States
$2	Thomas Jefferson	The signers of the Declaration of Independence
$5	Abraham Lincoln	The Lincoln Memorial
$10	Alexander Hamilton	The U.S. Treasury building
$20	Andrew Jackson	The White House
$50	Ulysses S. Grant	The U.S. Capitol
$100	Benjamin Franklin	Independence Hall

In this article, the author describes two types of "money personalities": the miser, the person who enjoys saving money, and the spendthrift, the person who enjoys spending.

Before you read, think about the following questions:

- Are you a miser or a spendthrift?
- What are some good reasons to save money?
- What are some good reasons to spend money?

Cultural Cues

Charles D'Orleans (1391–1465) A wealthy member of French royalty, held captive by the British; he was known for his poetry.

About the Author

Eric Tyson is a syndicated columnist, financial counselor and author of *Personal Finance for Dummies®*.

A Tale of Two Extremes
by Eric Tyson

When it comes to money, you're a hardworking miser, a free spirit or spendthrift, or something in between.

Misers

5 Some want to make and save a lot of money in order to retire early. I see people pursuing higher-paying and increasingly demanding careers to accomplish this goal. They make many personal sacrifices in exchange for income 10 today.

The problem is that tomorrow might not come. Even if all goes according to plan, will you know how to be happy when you're not working if you spend your entire life making 15 money? More importantly, who will be around to share your leisure time? One of the costs of engaging in an intense career is time spent away from friends and family. You may indeed realize your goal of retiring early, but you may 20 be putting off too much living today in expectation of living tomorrow.

As **Charles D'Orleans** said in 1465, "It's very well to be thrifty, but don't amass a hoard of regrets."

25 ## Spendthrifts

At the other extreme are those who live only for today. A friend of mine once said, "I'm not into **delayed gratification**[1]." *Shop until you drop* seems to be the motto of this personality 30 type. "Why bother saving when I might not be here tomorrow?" reason these people.

The danger of this approach is that tomorrow may come after all, and most people don't want to spend all their tomorrows working for 35 a living. The earlier neglect of saving, however, handicaps the possibility of *not* working when you are older.

A happy medium

Neither extreme is good, obviously.

40 You may be surprised to hear me say that if you must pick an extreme, I think it's better to pick the spendthrift approach. (Do I hear a collective sigh of relief?) As long as you have a financial safety net, a nest egg of some kind 45 or relatives or friends you can really count on, and you don't mind continuing to work (assuming your health allows), you should be okay. At least you're making use of your money and, hopefully, deriving value and pleasure from it.

50 The only difference between a person without savings or access to private healthcare and some homeless people is a few months of unemployment.

[1]delayed gratification = enjoying something at a later time

Postponing doing what you love and being
55 with people you love until retirement can be a
mistake. It may never come. Retirement can
be a great time for some people; for others, it is
a time of boredom, loneliness, and poor health.
You won't know what it will be like for you
60 until you get there. In the meantime, you need
to figure out where you stand financially regarding retirement planning. If you're like most
working people, you need to increase your savings rate for retirement.

Source: *Personal Finance for Dummies*

Check Your Comprehension

1. What are the advantages a miser has?

2. What are the disadvantages?

3. What are the advantages a spendthrift has?

4. What are the disadvantages?

5. What does the phrase "a happy medium" mean?

6. What does Tyson mean by "the only difference between a person without savings or access to private healthcare and some homeless people is a few months of unemployment"?

7. What does this quotation from Charles d'Orleans mean: "It's very well to be thrifty, but don't amass a hoard of regrets"?

8. Which extreme does Tyson think is better? Do you agree?

 READING

Find out more about **understanding from context** by looking in the Reference Guide to Reading Strategies on pages xii–xiv.

Understanding from Context

Find the following sentences in the reading and write down the line number where you find each one. Look at the text that surrounds it. Don't use your dictionary! From the context of the reading, explain what each sentence means.

1. Don't amass a hoard of regrets.

   Paragraph _____

   Meaning: _____

2. I'm not into delayed gratification.

   Paragraph _____

   Meaning: _____

3. Shop until you drop.

   Paragraph _____

   Meaning: _____

4. You should have a financial safety net.

Paragraph _____

Meaning: _____

5. Do you have a nest egg?

Paragraph _____

Meaning: _____

What information in the text gives you clues to the meaning of these sentences? Discuss your answers with a classmate.

VOCABULARY
Quantifiers

The following list contains words that show quantity. Choose the correct ones to put in the blanks in the sentences. Some may have more than one correct answer, although sometimes the different answers change the meaning of the sentence.

a lot of	*much*	*too many*	*a few*
lots of	*too much*	*all*	*some*
many	*most*	*few*	

1. Some people want to make _____ money.

2. Some people make _____ personal sacrifices to make money.

3. Some people put _____ emphasis on money.

4. _____ people don't want to work their entire life.

5. People don't want to spend _____ of their tomorrows working.

6. You should get _____ pleasure from your work.

7. The difference between _____ homeless people and people without _____ savings is _____ months of unemployment.

8. If you're like _____ people, you need to save _____ money for retirement.

THINK ABOUT IT

1. Are you a miser or a spendthrift? Which do you think is better?

2. What do you imagine retirement to be like? Do you look forward to it?

3. What is your favorite way to spend money?

Before You Read

Microsoft Corporation Financial Highlights, 1997
(in millions, except earnings per share, for the year ending June 30)

	1993	**1994**	**1995**	**1996**	**1997**
Revenue	$3,753	$4,649	$5,937	$8,671	$11,358
Net income	953	1,146	1,453	2,195	3,454
Return on revenue	25.4%	24.7%	24.5%	25.3%	30.4%
Total assets	3,805	5,363	7,210	10,093	14,387

Source: Adapted from information found at:
http://www.microsoft.com/msft/ar97/financial/highlights.htm

Watch the CNN video on Bill Gates.
Discuss these questions:

1. According to the report, how rich is Bill Gates?

2. Who is the richest American ever?

3. What did you learn about Bill Gates?

Discuss the chart in class.

- What do you think "net income" means?
- What does "total assets" mean?

In the following reading, the author discusses the life of Bill Gates, the Chairman of Microsoft, and one of the richest men in the world.

Before you read, think about the following questions:

- Have you heard of Bill Gates?
- Have you used Microsoft products?
- Is it possible to be "too rich"?

Seattle, Washington, home of Microsoft Corporation

Cultural Cues

Bellevue A city in Washington state, near Seattle.

Tiffany's A jewelry store known for fine and expensive items.

that eye of the camel thing A reference to a quotation from the Christian Bible: "It is easier for a camel to pass through the eye of a needle, than for a rich man to enter the kingdom of God."

USDA surplus commodities The U.S. Department of Agriculture is a government office that controls agricultural products and business. Surplus commodities are foods that there are too much of.

Times The *Seattle Times*, the paper in which this article appeared.

money does a body good This is a reference to some popular advertisements for milk, which told people "Milk does a body good."

government cheese This refers to a government program in which poor people were given free cheese each month.

About the Author

Jerry Large is a columnist for the *Seattle Times*, from which this column is taken.

BILL'S $50 BIL
BY ALL ACCOUNTS, A LOT OF DOUGH
BY JERRY LARGE

This week, Bill Gates is worth $50 billion and I'm not.

I don't **begrudge**[1] him the financial success. Why should I be jealous?

5   It is of course, my own fault that I am not the possessor of 50 billion dollars, just as it is your lack of initiative, or perhaps your contentment with a more **pedestrian portfolio**[2], that keeps you out of the billion-dollar club.

10   What would we do with 50 billion dollars, anyway?

Well, you and I, being socially conscious and caring people, would give it all away, wouldn't we? And by doing so we would prove 15 that the reason we didn't have billions before is that we never wanted billions.

But suppose we were shallow and self-absorbed.

I see swimming pools and beach vacations, 20 jets and yachts, island property and that ranch in New Mexico I've been thinking about.

A while back, *American* **Demographics**[3] magazine pawed through some statistics and discovered that rich people do find ways to 25 dispose of income.

[1]begrudge = deny

[2]pedestrian portfolio = average collection of savings and investments, one that doesn't produce large amounts of money. "Pedestrian" here means "everyday."

[3]demographics = the study of populations

How about a $55,000 trip around the world in a private supersonic Concorde, or some jewelry from **Tiffany's**?

Keith Ervin, a *Times* business reporter, did
30 a story last December on the recent influx of stores aimed at the sort of folks for whom a $100 bill looks like a penny.

He mentioned Barcelino, a **Bellevue** men's clothing store where a customer has spent
35 more than $23,000 in a single visit.

Lots of stores like that have located in Seattle or have plans to open a shop to sop up some of that money. He reported there are about 59,000 families around the Sound with at least
40 $1 million.

Even so, there is only so much stuff you can use.

Average folks spend 96 percent of annual after-tax income each year. The rich spend only
45 about two-thirds of their after-tax income each year, which means money keeps accumulating and they keep getting richer.

A million dollars is flea food next to the porterhouse steak Gates has. If you or I had
50 $50 billion, we could spend a million a year for 50,000 years. (Actually, we'd be spending only the interest, so we'd never run out of money.) Look at it another way: It is a $50,000–a-year salary for a million years.
55 Bill, a little pointer: Invest in some congressional friends. **Money does a body good.**

I know, I shouldn't go on like this about money. Money is evil, or lust for it is, anyway. There's **that eye of the camel thing**, and there
60 is always everyone's favorite money-can't-buy happiness examples, the Kennedys—wealth, fame, power, looks and misery.

But, hey, it beats starvation.

We are all mature enough to know that the
65 business of America is making green.

People don't flock here so that they can have the freedom to vote; they come to make money.

Money buys choices. People with money
70 have options when opportunities or problems arise.

Money also buys a little security. A lot of people in the middle class have a very loose grip on financial stability; a little bad luck and
75 it's back to the **government cheese**.

It wasn't until I tasted brie[4] that I realized that **USDA surplus commodities** weren't the last word in fine cuisine. I used to have a chip on my shoulder about the rich. Maybe I still
80 have a little of that, but I also think we've been lecturing the wrong people about the evils of money.

Poor people are a captive audience for people who believe in social justice and want a
85 world that is not driven by greed. Seems as though it is the wrong way around.

Tell rich people money is bad. Tell poor people to get some quick.

I'm not poor anymore, but I could always
90 use more money. I want everyone out there reading this to send me a dollar. Ask your friends and neighbors to send me a dollar and write to your relatives in Ohio and ask them to send money.
95 Remember, a newspaper column is software, too. I promise you that if I become a billionaire, I will not forget your help.

Oops. I think there might be some company rule against solicitations.[5] Never mind.

---

[4]brie = a type of fine French cheese
[5]solicitations = requests for money

Source: the *Seattle Times*

Check Your Comprehension

1. How has wealth affected the Seattle community, according to the writer?

2. What does "the business of America is making green" mean? What does "green" refer to?

3. What is the difference between the way the rich spend money and the way average people spend money, according to the reading?

4. What does "invest in some congressional friends" mean? What's another way of saying this?

5. What does the author mean when he says, "we've been lecturing the wrong people about the evils of money"?

6. What is the author's opinion of wealth? What sentences in the reading tell you that?

7. Why does the author say "a newspaper column is software too"?

8. What does this sentence mean: "Poor people are a captive audience for people who believe in social justice and want a world that is not driven by greed"?

**READING**

Find out more about **understanding humor** by looking in the Reference Guide to Reading Strategies on pages xii–xiv.

Understanding Humor

The tone of this article is humorous. However, the writer is also serious in some parts. Humor is often hard to understand in a second language. Read the sentences below, which are taken from the reading. Decide if the writer is being serious or humorous. Then try to describe why you feel that way. The first is done for you as an example.

1. It is of course, my own fault that I am not the possessor of 50 billion dollars, just as it is your lack of initiative, or perhaps your contentment with a more pedestrian portfolio, that keeps you out of the billion-dollar club.

   ☒ **Funny**   ☐ **Serious**

   I don't think he really believes that it's just "lack of initiative" that keeps people from being wealthy. He is exaggerating in order to be funny.

2. Well, you and I, being socially conscious and caring people, would give it all away, wouldn't we?

   ☐ **Funny**   ☐ **Serious**

3. He reported there are about 59,000 families around the Sound with at least $1 million.

   ☐ **Funny**   ☐ **Serious**

4. Average folks spend 96 percent of annual after-tax income each year.

☐ **Funny**   ☐ **Serious**

5. Money buys choices. People with money have options when opportunities or problems arise.

☐ **Funny**   ☐ **Serious**

6. Money also buys a little security.

☐ **Funny**   ☐ **Serious**

7. Ask your friends and neighbors to send me a dollar and write to your relatives in Ohio and ask them to send money.

☐ **Funny**   ☐ **Serious**

VOCABULARY
Idioms and Colloquial Language

This reading uses idioms and colloquial language. Complete the sentences using the **boldface** phrases below, taken from the reading.

1. If advertising is **aimed at** you, it _____ .

2. I have a **chip on my shoulder** about _____ .

3. A **captive audience** can't _____ .

4. A person who is **shallow and self-absorbed** would probably _____

   _____ .

5. If you **pawed through** a stack of magazines, you _____ .

6. My favorite way to **dispose of income** is _____ .

7. If people **flock** to the city, they _____ .

8. I think that _____ is **the last word in** _____ .

THINK ABOUT IT

1. The author says, "People don't flock here so that they can have the freedom to vote; they come to make money." Do you agree? Why or why not?

2. In the United States, it is usually considered impolite to talk about how much money you earn. Is this true in your country as well? What do you think of this practice?

3. The author says that money buys security. In what ways do you think this is true? Do you agree?

S Y N T H E S I S

Discussion and Debate

1. Would you rather work at a job you love, even if it didn't pay well, or a job you didn't like, but that paid a lot of money? Why?

2. Imagine you've won the lottery—$10,000,000. What are you going to do with the money? Save it or spend it? Or both? Will you quit school or your job? Why or why not?

3. There is a saying "Money can't buy happiness." Do you agree? Why or why not?

Writing Topics

1. In your journal, write about the job you would love to have. Consider more than just money—what kind of work would make you happy?

2. Do some research on the job you would love to have. Write a short report about the job, answering the following questions:

    Type of job:

    Average yearly salary:

    Education needed to get the job:

    Typical duties of the job:

    Typical work schedule of the job:

3. Is it better to save money or spend it? Write an essay in which you persuade your reader of your point of view. Use examples from your reading and from your own experience in your essay.

On Your Own

1. What agencies are available in your community to help the homeless? Do some research to find out.

2. Look in the job ads in your local newspaper. Find three that interest you and bring them to class to talk about. Why do you think they would be good jobs?

3. Interview three people on the topic of homelessness. Add more questions if you want.

   - Why do you think people become homeless?
   - What can people do to help the homeless?
   - Do you give homeless people money? Why or why not?

   Report your results to your class.

4. The following films deal with the subject of wealth or working. Watch one of them, and discuss it with your class.

The Money Pit	*Gung Ho*
Changing Places	*Melvin and Howard*
Annie	*It Could Happen to You*
Norma Rae	

A L M A N A C For additional cultural information, refer to the Almanac on pages 217–228. The Almanac contains lists of useful facts, maps, and other information to enhance your learning.

★★★

CHAPTER 3

Traditions

Every culture has traditions—in fact, traditions are what make one culture different from another. In the first part of this chapter, you will look at some traditions associated with the winter holidays in the United States. In the second part, you will read about some toys that have been traditional favorites with American children.

❄ Winter: Home for the Holidays ❄

Christmas has Christian origins, as the name of the holiday suggests.
In the United States it is also a national holiday. However, it is certainly not the
only important winter holidays. A variety of religions and cultures celebrate their
own special winter holidays. This section looks at one of these—an African-American
holiday called Kwanzaa.

Before You Read

Watch the CNN video on the celebration of Kwanzaa.

Discuss these questions:

1. How did Kwanzaa begin?

2. What are the reasons for the celebration?

3. How do people celebrate Kwanzaa?

Before you read, think about these questions:

- Do you celebrate a winter holiday? Which one?

- How do you celebrate this holiday?

- What other winter holidays do you know something about?

KWANZAA HISTORY

Kwanzaa is a cultural festival during which African-Americans celebrate and reflect upon their rich heritage as the products of two worlds. It begins December 26 and lasts for seven days. Kwanzaa was founded in 1966 by Dr. Maulana "Ron" Karenga, a college professor and African-American leader,
5   who believed that a special holiday could help African-Americans meet their goals of building strong families, learning about their history, and creating a sense of unity. After conducting extensive research in which he studied the festivals of many African groups of people, he decided that the new holiday should be a harvest or "first fruits" celebration, incorporating ideas
10 from many different harvest traditions. Kwanzaa is a Kiswahili word meaning "the first fruits of the harvest."

The East African language of Kiswahili was chosen as the official language of Kwanzaa because it is a non-tribal language spoken by a large portion of the African population. Also, its pronunciation is easy—the vowels
15 are pronounced like those in Spanish, and the consonants, for the most part, like those in English.

Kwanzaa is based on seven principles which are called Nguzo Saba. The principles are Umoja (Unity), Kujichagulia (Self-determination), Ujima (Collective Work and Responsibility), Ujamaa (Cooperative Economics),
20 Nia (Purpose), Kuumba (Creativity), and Imani (Faith). One principle is highlighted each day of the holiday.

In preparation for the celebration, a straw place mat (Mkeka) is placed on the table, along with a seven-candle candle holder (Kinara) with seven candles, one black (placed in the center), three red (on the right), and three
25 green (on the left). The black candle represents the African-American people, the red is for their struggles, and the green represents their hopes for the future. Other items placed on the table are a variety of fruit (Mazao), ears of corn (Vibunzi) representing the number of children in the family, gifts (Zawadi), and a communal unity cup (Kikombe Cha Umoja) for pouring
30 and sharing **libation**[1].

Each day of Kwanzaa, usually before the evening meal, family and friends gather around the table and someone lights a candle, beginning with the black. After that candles are lit alternately from left to right. While the candle is being lit, a principle is recited; then each person present takes a
35 turn to speak about the importance that principle has to him- or herself. Next the ceremony focuses on remembering those who have died. A selected

[1]libation = drinks

person pours water or juice from the unity cup into a bowl. That person then drinks from the cup and raises it high saying "Harambee" which means "Let's all pull together." All repeat "Harambee!" seven times and each person
40 drinks from the cup. Then names of African-American leaders and heroes are called out, and everyone reflects upon the great things these people did. The ceremony is followed by a meal, and then singing and perhaps listening to African music.

Source: *Win95 Magazine*

Check Your Comprehension

1. What does the word *kwanzaa* mean?

2. Why was the holiday Kwanzaa created?

3. What language is the word *kwanzaa* from?

4. What is the official language of Kwanzaa? Why was it chosen?

5. When did the holiday Kwanzaa begin?

6. What are the seven principles upon which Kwanzaa is based?

7. What is a "unity cup" and why is it used?

8. What does "the products of two worlds" mean in this reading?

9. What does "harambee" mean?

 READING

Find out more about **understanding processes** by looking in the Reference Guide to Reading Strategies on pages xii–xiv.

Understanding Processes

This reading describes the process of celebrating Kwanzaa. Review the reading and write the *16 steps* people take to celebrate Kwanzaa. (You may find you have a different number of steps, depending on how you combine certain procedures.)

Write these steps as instructions, using *imperative* verbs. Use "sequencing words" (such as *first, next, then,* etc. to show the order.) The first one is done for you.

Step 1: ___First, put a straw place mat (Mkeka) on the table.___

Step 2: _____

Step 3: _____

Step 4: _____

Step 5: _____

Step 6: _____

Step 7: _____

Step 8: _____

Step 9: _____

Step 10: _____

Step 11: _____

Step 12: _____

Step 13: _____

Step 14: _____

Step 15: _____

Step 16: _____

VOCABULARY
Using Translation

Sometimes, translating a word into your native language helps you to understand its meaning better. Look at these words and their translations into Kiswahili. Then, translate them into your own language.

The name of the principle	Translated into Kiswahili	Translated into your first language
1. Unity	_Umoja_	
2. Self-determination	_Kujichagulia_	
3. Collective Work and Responsibility	_Ujima_	
4. Cooperative Economics	_Ujamaa_	
5. Purpose	_Nia_	
6. Creativity	_Kuumba_	
7. Faith	_Imani_	

Talk to another student about your translations. Were they easy to do? Which ones were most difficult? Why?

THINK ABOUT IT

1. Kwanzaa is based on seven principles. The number seven, in fact, is important in many stories and customs. Can you think of any others? Does the number seven have any special significance in your culture?

2. Is Kwanzaa similar to any other holidays you know (in any culture)? Which ones? How is it similar? What are the differences?

3. Why do you think Kwanzaa is important to the African-American community?

Before You Read

Largest Department Store Chains in the United States

Store	Annual Sales
1. Sears Roebuck	$59,101,100,000
2. Wal-Mart Stores	55,483,800,000
3. Kmart	37,724,000,000
4. J.C. Penney	19,085,000,000
5. Dayton Hudson	17,927,000,000
6. May Department Stores	11,170,000,000
7. Woolworth	9,962,000,000
8. Federated Department Stores	7,079,900,000
9. R.H. Macy	6,648,900,000
10. Dillard Department Stores	4,883,200,000

Source: Blackburn Marketing Services

Some American department stores take in half of their annual sales during the Christmas shopping season (Thanksgiving through New Year's Day). This is because Americans spend so much money on Christmas, Hannukah, and Kwanzaa presents.

• What holidays do you celebrate by giving gifts?
• How important are holiday gifts to you?
• How much do you spend on holiday presents for family and friends?

The following story has been slightly simplified from its original version.

Cultural Cues

magi   The three kings who brought precious gifts to Christ when he was born.

the gift of the magi   A special way of saying "the Christmas gift."

Queen of Sheba and King Solomon   Sheba was an ancient country of southern Arabia. Today it is called Yemen. Its people were known for their wealth. In the Old Testament of the Judeo-Christian Bible, the Queen of Sheba visited King Solomon.

Coney Island An amusement park in New York.

chorus girl A young woman who sings and dances in the theater, but is not one of the stars.

Broadway A popular shopping and theatre street in New York.

About the Author

O. Henry was born William Sydney Porter in 1862 in Greensboro, North Carolina. He was brought up in the South during the depression after the Civil War. He held different jobs before becoming a teller in the First National Bank. He was put in prison for stealing money in 1898. He started writing short stories in prison under his pseudonym, O. Henry. After his release, he moved to New York City, and wrote the first of his many books, *Cabbages and Kings*, in 1904. His stories provide a romantic and humorous treatment of everyday life. They are also known for their use of coincidence and trick endings. He died in 1910.

by O. Henry The Gift of the Magi

One dollar and eighty-seven cents. That was all. And sixty cents of it was in pennies. Pennies saved one and two at a time by bargaining with the grocer and the vegetable man and
5 the butcher until one's cheeks burned with the silent guilt of being cheap. Three times Della counted it. One dollar and eighty-seven cents. And the next day would be Christmas.

There was clearly nothing to do but flop
10 down on the **shabby**[1] little couch and howl. So Della did it. Which makes one believe the fact that life is made up of sobs, sniffles, and smiles, with sniffles the most common.

While the mistress of the home is gradually
15 going from sobbing to sniffling, take a look at

[1]shabby = old and worn out

the home. A furnished flat at $8 per week. In the entryway below was a letter-box into which no letter would go, and a doorbell which no finger could cause to ring. Also there was a
20 card on it with the name "Mr. James Dillingham Young."

The "Dillingham" had been added during a former period of prosperity when its possessor was being paid $30 per week. Now, when the
25 income was shrunk to $20, though, they were thinking seriously of contracting it to a modest "D." But whenever Mr. James Dillingham Young came home and reached his flat above he was called "Jim" and greatly hugged by Mrs. James
30 Dillingham Young, already introduced to you as Della. Which is all very good.

Della finished her cry and attended to her cheeks with some powder. She stood by the

window and looked out dully at a gray cat walk-
35 ing a gray fence in a gray backyard. Tomorrow
would be Christmas Day, and she had only
$1.87 with which to buy Jim a present. She had
been saving every penny she could for months,
with this result. Twenty dollars a week doesn't
40 go far. Expenses had been greater than she had
calculated. They always are. Only $1.87 to buy
a present for Jim. Her Jim. Many a happy hour
she had spent planning for something nice for
him. Something fine and rare and silver—
45 something worthy of the honor of being owned
by Jim.

There were narrow mirrors between the
windows of the room. Perhaps you have seen
such mirrors in a cheap flat. A very thin person
50 may, by observing his reflection in a rapid sequence of these long narrow mirrors, get a
fairly accurate reflection of his looks. Della,
being slender, had mastered the art.

Suddenly she whirled from the window and
55 stood before the mirror. Her eyes were shining
brilliantly, but her face had lost its color within
twenty seconds. Rapidly she pulled down her
hair and let it fall to its full length.

Now, there were two possessions of the
60 James Dillingham Youngs in which they both
took great pride. One was Jim's gold watch that
had been his father's and his grandfather's. The
other was Della's hair. Had the **Queen of
Sheba** lived in the flat across from theirs, Della
65 would have let her hair hang out the window
some day to dry just to make the Queen's jewels
and gifts less valuable. Had **King Solomon**
been the janitor, with all his treasures piled up
in the basement, Jim would have pulled out his
70 watch every time he passed, just to see him
pull at his beard from envy.

So now Della's beautiful hair fell about her
flowing and shining like a **cascade**[2] of brown
waters. It reached below her knee and was
75 almost like a dress. And then she did it up again
nervously and quickly. Once she fumbled for a
minute and stood still while a tear or two
splashed on the worn red carpet.

She put on her old brown jacket; she put
80 on her old brown hat. With a whirl of skirts
and with the brilliant sparkle still in her eyes,
she fluttered out the door and down the stairs
to the street.

Where she stopped the sign said: "Madame
85 Sofronie. Hair Goods of All Kinds." One flight
up Della ran, and collected herself, panting.
Madame, large, too white, chilly, hardly looked
the "Sofronie."

"Will you buy my hair?" asked Della.
90 "I buy hair," said Madame. "Take yer hat off
and let's have a look at it."

The brown cascade rippled down.

"Twenty dollars," said Madame, lifting the
hair with a skilled hand.
95 "Give it to me quick," said Della.

Oh, and the next two hours flew by on rosy
wings. Forget the fancy **metaphor**[3]. She was
ransacking[4] the stores for Jim's present.

She found it at last. It surely had been made
100 for Jim and no one else. There was no other
like it in any of the stores, and she had turned
all of them inside out. It was a platinum fob
chain simple and pure in design, showing its
value by substance alone and not by **ornate**[5]
105 decoration—as all good things should do. It
was even worthy of The Watch. As soon as she
saw it she knew that it must be Jim's. It was
like him. Quietness and value—the description
applied to both. They took twenty-one dollars
110 for it, and she hurried home with the remaining
87 cents. With that chain on his watch, Jim
would be eager to check the time in any company. As wonderful as the watch was, he sometimes looked at it secretly because of the old
115 leather strap that he used in place of a chain.

When Della reached home her excitement
changed a little to reason. She got out her curl-

[2]cascade = waterfall

[3]metaphor = a type of comparison; in this case Della's
hair is a cascade

[4]ransack = search aggressively for something

[5]ornate = fancy, very decorative

ing irons and went to work trying to fix her hair, which was now a mess made by generosity
120 added to love. Which is always a tremendous task, dear friends—a gigantic task.

Within forty minutes her head was covered with tiny, close-lying curls that made her look wonderfully like a schoolboy. She looked at
125 her reflection in the mirror long, carefully, and critically.

"If Jim doesn't kill me," she said to herself, "before he takes a second look at me, he'll say I look like a **Coney Island chorus girl.** But
130 what could I do—oh! what could I do with a dollar and eighty-seven cents?"

At 7 o'clock the coffee was made and the frying-pan was on the back of the stove hot and ready to cook the chops.

135 Jim was never late. Della held the fob chain in her hand and sat on the corner of the table near the door that he always entered. Then she heard his step on the stairs down on the first floor, and she turned white for just a moment.
140 She had a habit of saying a little silent prayer about the simplest everyday things, and now she whispered: "Please God, make him think I am still pretty."

The door opened and Jim stepped in and
145 closed it. He looked thin and very serious. Poor fellow, he was only twenty-two—and to be burdened with a family! He needed a new overcoat and he had no gloves.

Jim stopped inside the door, as still as a
150 dog at the scent of bird. He stared at Della, and there was a look in them that she could not understand, and it scared her. It was not anger, nor surprise, nor disapproval, nor horror, nor any of the feelings that she had been
155 prepared for. He simply stared at her with that peculiar expression on his face.

Della wriggled off the table and went for him.

"Jim, darling," she cried, "don't look at me
160 that way. I had my hair cut off and sold because I couldn't have lived through Christmas without giving you a present. It'll grow out again— you won't mind, will you? I just had to do it.

My hair grows awfully fast. Say 'Merry Christ-
165 mas!' Jim, and let's be happy. You don't know what a nice—what a beautiful, nice gift I've got for you."

"You've cut off your hair?" asked Jim, slowly, as if he had not understood, even
170 though he had thought hard about it.

"Cut it off and sold it," said Della. "Don't you like me just as well, anyhow? I'm me without my hair, ain't I?"

Jim looked about the room curiously.

175 "You say your hair is gone?" he said, seeming almost stupid.

"Don't look for it," said Della. "It's sold, I tell you—sold and gone, too. It's Christmas Eve, boy. Be good to me, for I sold it for you.
180 Maybe the hairs of my head were numbered," she went on with sudden serious sweetness, "but nobody could ever count my love for you. Shall I put the chops on, Jim?"

Jim seemed quickly to wake out of his
185 trance. He hugged his Della. For ten seconds let's not watch them. Eight dollars a week or a million a year—what is the difference? A mathematician or a scholar would give you the wrong answer. The **magi** brought valuable gifts,
190 but that was not among them. This dark statement will be illuminated later on.

Jim drew a package from his overcoat pocket and threw it upon the table.

"Don't make any mistake, Dell," he said,
195 "about me. I don't think there's a haircut that could make me like my girl any less. But if you'll unwrap that package you may see why I acted like I did."

White fingers tore at the string and paper.
200 And then a happy scream of joy; and then, alas! a quick change to tears and crying, requiring the immediate comfort of her husband.

For there lay The Combs—the set of combs that Della had admired in a **Broadway** window.
205 Beautiful combs, pure tortoise shell, with jewelled **rims**[6]—just the right color for her beautiful vanished hair. They were expensive combs,

[6]rims = the outside part of something

she knew, and her heart had yearned for them without believing she would ever have them. 210 And now, they were hers, but the hair that should have held the beautiful combs was gone.

But she held them tightly, and she looked up with sad eyes and a smile and say: "My hair 215 grows so fast, Jim!"

And then Della leaped up like a little cat and cried, "Oh, oh!"

Jim had not yet seen his beautiful present. She held it out to him eagerly with her open 220 hand. The dull precious metal seemed to flash with a reflection of her bright spirit.

"Isn't it wonderful, Jim? I hunted all over town to find it. You'll have to look at the time a hundred times a day now. Give me your 225 watch. I want to see how it looks on it."

Instead of obeying, Jim sat down on the couch, leaned back, and smiled.

"Dell," said he, "let's put our Christmas presents away and keep 'em a while. They're too 230 nice to use right now. I sold the watch to get the money to buy your combs. And now suppose you put the chops on."

The magi, as you know, were wise men—wonderfully wise men—who brought gifts to 235 the baby Jesus. They invented the art of giving Christmas presents. Being wise, their gifts were wise ones, perhaps ones you could exchange if you got two. And here I have told you the dull story of two foolish children in a flat who 240 most unwisely sacrificed for each other the greatest treasures of their house. But in a last word to the wise of these days let it be said that of all who give gifts, these two were the wisest. Of all who give and receive gifts, such 245 as they are wisest. Everywhere they are wisest. They are the magi.

Check Your Comprehension

1. What sort of apartment did the Youngs live in?

2. What is the reason that Della is crying at the beginning of the story?

3. Why are they thinking of changing the name plate to read "D." instead of "Dillingham"?

4. How does Della solve her problem?

5. How does Jim react to seeing Della's hair?

6. How does Jim get the money for Della's gift?

7. Why is this story called "The Gift of the Magi"?

 **READING**

Find out more about **summarizing** by looking in the Reference Guide to Reading Strategies on pages xii–xiv.

Summarizing

Summarizing a short story can help you understand what details were important to you. Using the space below (and no more!) summarize "The Gift of the Magi." Then compare your summary to one that a classmate wrote. How are the details different? What did you focus on? Discuss these questions with your partner.

_____

_____

_____

_____

_____

VOCABULARY
Word Search

The following words are found in the reading. Begin by writing their meanings in the blanks. Then circle them again in the following puzzle. The letters in these words are written horizontally, vertically, left to right, and right to left. The first word in the puzzle is done for you.

butcher _____

cascade _____

cheap _____

janitor _____

magi _____

metaphor _____

ornate _____

peculiar _____

prayer _____

prosperity _____

ripple _____

sacrifice _____

scholar _____

shabby _____

sniffles _____

sobs _____

sparkle _____

tortoise _____

yearn _____

```
s  o  b  s  a  q  x  m  u  p  o  m  o  f  o
p  r  r  e  c  i  f  i  r  c  a  s  f  k  r
a  n  e  o  k  s  f  o  a  g  k  a  b  n  s
r  a  l  o  h  c  s  n  i  f  f  l  e  s  o
k  t  m  f  n  p  i  z  l  o  v  f  c  x  l
l  e  s  p  e  e  a  e  u  b  k  h  u  v  u
e  k  o  r  a [b  u  t  c  h  e  r] q  h  m
e  s  i  o  t  r  o  t  e  a  f  p  s  l  d
w  t  v  z  e  q  g  d  p  m  a  l  l  f  w
y  q  o  y  j  j  a  n  i  t  o  r  f  r  y
i  b  a  b  b  c  l  r  z  i  r  i  x  b  h
o  r  b  d  s  z  e  a  u  f  l  p  x  j  d
p  u  x  a  a  q  j  e  h  w  g  p  u  u  r
n  b  c  m  h  j  r  y  h  f  v  l  z  i  o
w  z  r  f  h  s  w  y  l  l  h  e  b  t  j
```

√ ~~butcher~~
cascade
cheap
fob
janitor
magi
metaphor
ornate
peculiar
prayer
prosperity
ripple
sacrifice
scholar
shabby
sniffles
sobs
sparkle
tortoise
yearn

THINK ABOUT IT

1. What is the best gift you have ever received? Why was it so special?

2. Why does the author say that "these two were the wisest" at the end of the story?

3. How do you think this story shows the "true spirit of Christmas"?

PART TWO

Childhood: A Child at Heart

Childhood is a time of traditions. Traditional songs,
games, and toys play an important part in the life of
the Ammerican Child.

Before You Read

In this essay, the author talks about his first bicycle.

Before you read, think about the following questions:

- Have you ever owned a bicycle? Do you remember your first bicycle?
- Why do you think bicycles are so important to children?

Cultural Cues   *paper route* The route refers to the streets that the delivery person travels
to deliver the newspapers.

About the Author   Brian Lonsway lives in Waterville, Ohio. He collects old bicycles.

Western Flyer
by Brian Lonsway

It all started in Toledo, Ohio on the evening of August 11, 1951. That was when Dad gave me and my sister the most wonderful surprise of our young lives—new bikes!

We'd always been happy with the secondhand or homemade toys we'd
5 been given, but this was something special. Even the **serial number**[1] of my bike—A59296A—remains forever locked in my mind!

I was 11 years old then, and I immediately took off to show friends my new "machine". Every day I rode the bike to school—and everywhere else. When I got a **paper route,** I made a box to hold the papers on the luggage
10 rack.

Although it seemed our bikes were built to last forever, that didn't stop my buddies and me from constantly **dismantling**[2] them for unneeded maintenance.

Such Shining Times

15 Over the years, our bikes wore assorted reflectors, mud flaps, handlebar streamers and even hubcaps. Every summer, we stripped them down (for speed, of course) and removed tanks, fenders and all the accessories. With handlebars turned upside down, they were now "racers".

Sometimes I wonder how we survived when I recall the "backward races"
20 we had. Sitting on the handlebars and facing the rear, I'd pedal furiously while looking over my shoulder. All in all, I did pretty well . . . I remember only three major crack-ups.

Once, the bike went sailing over my head when I hit a curb. Another time, I took a dramatic "header" when the front fender caught a tree support
25 wire. And I well remember the nasty cut I got while trying to ride the bike standing on the crossbar.

I'll also never forget the longest trip I took on my bike. One night when I was 13, I decided to run away from home . . . sort of. After pedaling for what seemed forever, I found myself in a place with lots of pavement and
30 strange-colored lights.

The sound of an airplane finally confirmed the realization that I'd strayed onto the tarmac of the Toledo airport, 11 miles from home.

---

[1]serial number = the special number which is different for every item a manufacturer sells
[2]dismantling = taking something apart into separate pieces

Caught in the glare of an airplane's landing lights and scared that the police would soon be looking for me, I turned off my headlight and somehow
35 managed to find my way back home using dark country roads.

Winter Pedal Pushers

We loved our bikes so much that, in snowy weather, we'd laboriously thread heavy twine around the tires to create "snow chains". Try topping that for "**nerdiness**"³!
40 The only time in my life that my trusty Western Flyer got out of my sight was a brief period in the late 60s when I loaned it to Dad, then living in Florida. When I got the bike back from him, I was a little miffed to find he'd repainted it.

So what if the old paint had been a little thin because of all my polishing?
45 At least he got the color scheme right, even if the red is a little off. And now that Dad is gone, I have little inclination to change it, since the paint job reminds me of him.

Besides, the original decal is still there under the paint, and some of the old color can still be seen. Maybe someday my son will restore the old bike
50 to its original glory.

Yes, I still have my old Western Flyer. I'm also living in a house built in 1835. I drive a 1961 Ford Sunliner and take to the water in a 1955 Century Resorter speedboat.

Source: *Reminisce Magazine*   What can I say? I've seen the past, and it still works!

Check Your Comprehension

1. What kinds of gifts did the author get before he got his first bicycle?

2. What kinds of accidents did the author have with his bicycle?

3. What's a "backwards race"?

4. Why was the author upset that his father repainted the bike?

5. Why won't he repaint the bicycle now?

6. What was the longest trip the author ever took on his bike?

³nerdiness = a "nerd" is derogatory term for an uninteresting person who is extremely interested in an unusual hobby

READING

Find out more about **understanding examples** by looking in the Reference Guide to Reading Strategies on pages xii–xiv.

Understanding Examples

The author uses many examples to support his main ideas. List the examples that are used for each idea listed below. The first one is done for you.

1. The bicycle was the most special gift ever.

   Example: ___He even remembers the serial number: A59296A.___

2. He rode the bike everywhere.

   To _____,

   to _____,

   and to _____ .

3. He loved making changes to his bike.

   He made _____.

   He also put _____, _____, _____,

   and _____ on the bike.

4. He got in accidents with the bike.

   Example 1. _____

   Example 2. _____

   Example 3. _____

5. Even the paint was important.

   First _____,

   second _____,

   and finally, _____ .

6. The author likes old things.

   His bike was made _____

   _____ .

   His house was built _____

   _____ .

   His car is _____

   _____ .

   His boat is _____

   _____ .

VOCABULARY
Bicycle Words

Look at the following drawing. Label each part on the bike.

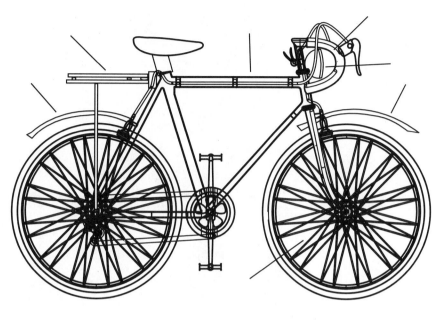

handlebar	*crossbar*
fender	*spokes*
headlight	*mudflap*
luggage rack	

THINK ABOUT IT

1. Why do you think the name of the bike, "Western Flyer," is important?

2. Bicycling is not a common form of transportation in the United States. Why do you think this is true?

3. Interview one of your classmates about his or her experience with bicycles. Think of three questions to ask him or her. One of them might be "When did you get your first bicycle?"

4. Do you have a bicycle now? How often do you use it?

Before You Read

Macy's City Shopper Barbie

The Barbie Doll became an important American toy in the 1950s. This doll is still very popular today.

The following reading is a collection of short writings about memories of Barbie. In it, both men and women talk about Barbie's role in their lives.

Before you read, think about the following questions:

• Have you ever seen or owned a Barbie Doll?

• Is there a doll or other toy that has been popular for a long time in your culture?

Cultural Cues

Ken doll Barbie's doll boyfriend.

Epcot Center Part of Disney World in which important scientific and cultural items are displayed.

Dream House A doll house made for Barbie.

Lake Shasta A large lake in Northern California.

Partridge Family A television show featuring a family that is also a rock and roll band. This show was popular in the early 1970s.

Donny and Marie   Referring to Donny and Marie Osmond, of the Osmond family. The Osmonds were a singing family popular in the late 1960s and early 1970s.

Brady Bunch   A 1970s television show with an idealized American family.

Mattel   The name of the toy company that makes Barbie and Ken dolls.

Macy's   A large department store.

Safeway   A large grocery store chain.

Madonna   A popular American singer.

G.I. Joe   A soldier doll, usually played with by boys.

Barbie Stories

From Mrs. Brown, 48

As one of the first groups of children to have Barbies, here's what I remember:

- Spending many hours in my cousin's backyard in the summer playing with our Barbies.
- Not liking the heavy makeup she wore in the beginning. I'm glad they changed that!
- My grandmother saying, "She certainly is healthy!"
- Wishing that I would look "healthy" someday; now I'm glad I don't.
- Wishing I had clothes like Barbie's—and the accessories were great!
- Thinking that Ken was really a sponger—why doesn't he have the car, condo, or gym equipment? I can't even find shoes for my niece's **Ken doll** collection!

From Margo T., 24

When I was about 7 or 8 years old, I got a Barbie for Christmas, even though I had not wanted one. She had only one dress, and the only accessory she had was a swimming pool. My parents couldn't afford much more. The pool was so difficult to put together that I was never able to do it right. It had a slide that the doll wouldn't slide down: she'd always fall off. Barbie could not swim in this pool either, because it was smaller than she was. If you put her in the pool, she fell over. I played with the pool for approximately twenty minutes before deciding it wasn't fun. In fact, I hated it! Furthermore, I hated the name "Barbie" too.

When I was about 9 or 10, my friend Sally and I created a Barbie "McDonald's." We used my one old Barbie and her collection of ten Barbies and Kens. They were the waiters and customers.

I still have a Barbie, though I'm 23. I dyed her hair purple, cut it, and made it into a mohawk. She wears a leather jacket, and she has a black tattoo. She is one of my most treasured toys.

From Barbie R., 40

I've always had Barbies. I really am a Barbie, and I live a Barbie life. My husband's name is even Ken! I loved that doll. However, then I

went to Disneyland and met the "Barbie" there. She was a loser! She wasn't perfect, not even
50 pretty. And Ken . . . he was a disappointment, too!

I used to chew on my Barbie's hands and blame it on my dog, whose name was Ken. We painted a big box to make our own **Dream
55 House,** since we couldn't afford the real one. We built a pool in the sand on **Lake Shasta** in California and pretended Barbie was so rich that she had her own pool and beach. Finally, I got the Barbie Dream Condo (with the eleva-
60 tor) for $1.00 at a garage sale.

The worst experience of my life was when our house burned down. I lost all of my Barbies and **the Partridge Family, Donny and Marie,** and **Brady Bunch** dolls. This event made
65 me the collector that I am today.

From Ken B., 19

I don't have many memories of Barbie, but I do remember that when my sister Sally played with Barbie, I had a Superman doll. So I wanted
70 to play with Sally and her Barbie, since she had the Barbie Van. Superman could take a nap, watch TV, cook some dinner, and then go out to fight evil! The problem was, he was about an inch shorter than all the Barbie dolls, so he
75 didn't exactly fit in. He's the superhero, but Barbie made him look like a little kid!

From Kathy S., 37

My sister and I never had many Barbie accessories or furniture. We didn't have enough money
80 to buy them. We used things that we found around our house. An empty shoe box was her bathtub. Those charm bracelets that were popular a few years ago became toys for Barbie's children. Back then, **Mattel** didn't sell
85 dishes or food for Barbie, so my sister and I would look through the Sunday paper for **Macy's** or **Safeway** advertisements and cut out pictures of food and dishes. Barbie and her friends would have a grand meal! I tell you, my
90 Barbie had a life of luxury! I had an electric hair curler and decided to try it on Barbie's hair. It burned it, so I cut it off and called her **Madonna** because she looked like her.

From Velma F., 28

95 When I was a little girl I cut off my Barbie's hair, and thought it was the coolest thing. I cut it straight across, a bob, like the cuts that were popular in the eighties. Then I cut off the hair of my sister's Barbie. I left it long on one side,
100 but cut it short on the other. Needless to say, my mom didn't like my hairdressing hobby and yelled at me. I still don't get it!

From Paul T., 21

My best memory of Barbie was when I put all
105 my **G.I. Joes** in my sisters' Barbie Camper. Then, I rolled it off the roof, and watched the camper break into a thousand pieces when it hit the driveway. The G.I. Joes sailed through the air. My sisters were so mad, and I was
110 grounded for two weeks.

Check Your Comprehension

1. What are some accessories that are made for Barbie?

2. What other dolls are named in the reading?

3. What activities or games seem to be popular with the children who play with Barbie?

4. How did the boys play with dolls in these passages?

5. What was the problem with Ken B.'s Superman doll?

READING

Find out more about **scanning** by looking in the Reference Guide to Reading Strategies on pages xii–xiv.

Scanning

Scanning means going over an article quickly to look for specific information. Scan the reading again, and answer the following questions.

1. Who is the oldest respondent? _____

2. Who had the most Barbies? _____

3. Who has a husband named Ken? _____

4. How many of the writers cut their Barbie's hair? _____

5. How many different accessories are mentioned? _____

6. Which male dolls are mentioned? _____, _____,

   and _____ .

VOCABULARY
Slang and Colloquial Language

Review the reading to see if you understand what the following boldfaced words mean. Discuss their meaning with your classmates. Then, complete the following sentences to show that you understand them.

1. John is a real **sponger;** he _____ .

2. A **loser** _____ .

3. My mother **grounded** me for _____ because I _____

   _____ .

4. I had the **coolest** idea today! I decided to _____ .

5. **I don't get it!** _____ .

THINK ABOUT IT

1. Whose story did you like the best? Why?

2. Do you have a Barbie Story (or a similar story about another toy)?

3. Today Barbie is controversial. This is because many people feel that she presents an unrealistic image of a woman. A new Barbie has a wider waist, wears flat shoes, and has a different face. What do you think of this controversy?

S Y N T H E S I S

Discussion and Debate

1. Many people say that Christmas is too commercial in America. They feel that people focus on buying and selling gifts more than on the spirit of the season. How does this idea fit into other ideas you have about American culture?

2. Why do you think holidays are important to people? Are they more important to adults or to children?

3. Think of another question to ask classmates about the ideas in this chapter.

Writing Topics

1. In your journal, write about some memories from childhood: your first bike, an important birthday, a favorite toy. Why do you think these memories are important to you?

2. Look up the following holidays, and write a short report on one of them:

   Kwanzaa   *Hannukah*   *Ramadan*

3. Write about the holiday that is most important in your culture. In your essay, discuss the following:
   a. when it is celebrated   **d.** who celebrates it
   b. its origin   **e.** special customs
   c. traditional foods

On Your Own

1. Go to a toy store and look at the toys that are popular today. Make notes and report back to the class.

2. Find someone who celebrates a holiday that you don't celebrate. Interview that person about the holiday. Also ask him or her about childhood memories of this holiday.

3. Take a poll of ten people about their childhood toys. Ask them these questions, and add some of your own:
   - What was your favorite childhood toy?
   - Do you still have that toy?
   - If not, what happened to it?
   - What kinds of games did you play as a child?

★★

A L M A N A C For additional cultural information, refer to the Almanac on pages 217–228. The Almanac contains lists of useful facts, maps, and other information to enhance your learning.

★★★

CHAPTER 4

People

The way that people treat each other is different in different cultures. This chapter looks at how Americans interact with their friends and their families.

PART ONE

Friends: A Friend In Need

Friendships exist in every culture. However, the character of friendships is different in each culture. This section takes a look at the character of American friendships.

Before You Read

The following reading is about friendships between men and women.

Before you read this essay, think about the following questions:

- Do you think men and women can be "just friends"?
- Who is your "best" friend?

 **READING**

Find out more about **skimming** by looking in the Reference Guide to Reading Strategies on pages xii–xiv.

Skimming

Skimming means reading something quickly to get the main idea. Before you read the article carefully, take no more than two minutes to skim the article. Then answer the questions below:

1. What is the main idea of the article? _____

_____

_____

2. What are the differences between men and women, according to the article? _____

_____

_____

3. Who is the center of a little girl's life? _____

_____

_____

Cultural Cues

Debbie Reynolds An actor who was popular in the 1950s and 1960s; she is best known for her part as Cathy Selden in *Singin' in the Rain.*

Dick Van Dyke A popular entertainer who had a television show in the 1950s and 60s called *The Dick Van Dyke Show.* He has been in many movies and television shows, including *Diagnosis Murder.*

About the Author

Deborah Tannen is a professor of linguistics at Georgetown University in Washington, D.C. She has written many books and articles, some of which have appeared in *The New York Times Magazine, Vogue, New York* Magazine, and *The Washington Post.* She lives in Washington, D.C.

by Deborah Tannen You Just Don't Understand

Once again, the seeds of women's and men's styles are sown in the ways they learn to use language while growing up. In our culture, most people, but especially women, look to their closest relationships as havens in a hostile world. The center of a little girl's social life is her best friend. Girls'
5 friendships are made and maintained by telling secrets. For grown women too, the **essence**[1] of friendship is talk, telling each other what they're thinking and feeling, and what happened that day: who was at the bus stop, who called, what they said, how that made them feel. When asked who their best friends are, most women name other women they talk to regularly.
10 When asked the same question, most men will say it's their wives. After that, many men name other men with whom they do things such as play tennis or baseball (but never just sit and talk) or a chum from high school whom they haven't spoken to in a year.

When **Debbie Reynolds** complained that **Dick Van Dyke** didn't tell her
15 anything, and he protested that he did, both were right. She felt he didn't tell her anything because he didn't tell her the fleeting thoughts and feelings he experienced throughout the day—the kind of talk she would have with her best friend. He didn't tell her these things because to him they didn't seem like anything to tell. He told her anything that seemed important—
20 anything he would tell his friends.

Men and women often have their different ideas of what's important—and at what point "important" topics should be raised. A woman told me, with lingering **incredulity**[2], of a conversation with her boyfriend. Knowing he had seen his friend Oliver, she asked, "What's new with Oliver?" He replied,
25 "Nothing." But later in the conversation it came out that Oliver and his girlfriend had decided to get married. "That's nothing?" the woman gasped in frustration and disbelief.

For men, "Nothing" may be a ritual response at the start of a conversation. A college woman missed her brother but rarely called him because she
30 found it difficult to get talk going. A typical conversation began with her asking, "What's up with you?" and his replying, "Nothing." Hearing his "Nothing" as meaning "There is nothing personal I want to talk about," she supplied talk by filling him in on her news and eventually hung up in frustration. But when she thought back, she remembered that later in the conversation he
35 had mumbled, "Christie and I got into another fight." This came so late and so low that she didn't pick up on it. And he was probably equally frustrated that she didn't.

[1]essence = basic quality
[2]incredulity = astonishment; state of being unsure

Source: *You Just Don't Understand*

40 Many men honestly do not know what women want, and women honestly do not know why men find what they want so hard to comprehend and deliver.

Check Your Comprehension

1. How are men's and women's friendships different, according to the author?

2. According to Tannen, how do men and women define "important" differently?

3. Who is a man likely to say is his best friend?

4. When a man says, "nothing," what might he really mean, according to the author?

5. What is the most important part of women's friendships, according to the reading?

VOCABULARY Using New Words

Look up the words below. Draw a line from each word at the left to the word or phrase at the right that most closely matches its meaning.

1. sow	**A.** brief
2. haven	**B.** disbelief
3. hostile	**C.** formal
4. fleeting	**D.** gulp
5. incredulity	**E.** murmur
6. gasp	**F.** plant
7. ritual	**G.** restrained
8. mumble	**H.** shelter
9. frustrated	**I.** unfriendly

Now, choose three of these words and write a sentence using each of them .

1. _____

_____

2. _____

_____

3. _____

_____

THINK ABOUT IT

1. Tannen says that American girls' friendships are very important. Is this true in your culture as well?

2. Do you agree with the author's last sentence in this essay? Why or why not?

3. Brainstorm with a partner or on your own. Make a list of three other things you have noticed about communication between men and women.

   1. _____

   2. _____

   3. _____

   Discuss these differences in class. Why do you think these differences exist?

Before You Read

This reading is a poem by one of the most important American poets, Robert Frost. In this poem, there is a line that is often repeated in American life: "Good fences make good neighbors."

Before you read the poem, think about the following questions:

- Do you enjoy poetry?
- Have you heard of Robert Frost before?
- What do you think "Good fences make good neighbors" means?

This poem may contain some words or phrases that are new to you. Read it slowly and think about the meaning of these words and phrases. You should read the poem at least twice.

Cultural Cues

wall To understand the poem, it's helpful to understand the sort of wall that the poet is describing. It is a wall made of stones, which creates a low fence around the owner's property, and is common in the northeastern part of the United States. (See photo above.)

About the Author

 Watch the CNN video on Robert Frost's farm.

Discuss these questions:

1. Where is Robert Frost's farm?

2. Which two states did Robert Frost think were the best in the U.S.?

3. Which President did Robert Frost write a poem for?

4. What did you learn about Robert Frost?

Robert Frost was born in 1874, in San Francisco, California. He studied at Harvard and became a teacher, shoemaker, and farmer before going to England (1912–15). While he was in England, he published *A Boy's Will* (1913) and *North of Boston* (1914), which brought him international fame. Back in the United States he taught at Amherst College and the University of Michigan. His book *New Hampshire* (1923) won the Pulitzer Prize, as did his first *Collected Poems* in 1930 and *A Further Range*, (1936). A last collection, *In the Clearing*, appeared in 1962. At the time of his death, he was regarded as the unofficial poet laureate of the United States.

by Robert Frost MENDING WALL

Something there is that doesn't love a wall,
That sends the **frozen-ground-swell**[1] under it,
And spills the upper boulders in the sun,
And makes gaps even two can pass abreast.
5 The work of hunters is another thing:
I have come after them and made repair
Where they have left not one stone on a stone,
But they would have the rabbit out of hiding,
To please the yelping dogs. The gaps I mean,
10 No one has seen them made or heard them made,
But at spring mending-time we find them there.
I let my neighbor know beyond the hill;
And on a day we meet to walk the line
And set the wall between us once again.
15 We keep the wall between us as we go.

[1]frozen-ground-swell = Pieces of earth move upward as the ground freezes in winter.

To each the boulders that have fallen to each.
And some are loaves and some so nearly balls
We have to use **a spell**[2] to make them balance:
'Stay where you are until our backs are turned!'
20 We wear our fingers rough with handling them.
Oh, just another kind of out-door game,
One on a side. It comes to little more:
There where it is we do not need the wall:
He is all pine and I am apple orchard.
25 My apple trees will never get across
And eat the cones under his pines, I tell him.
He only says, 'Good fences make good neighbors'.
Spring is the mischief in me, and I wonder
If I could put a notion in his head:
30 'Why do they make good neighbors? Isn't it
Where there are cows?
But here there are no cows.
Before I built a wall I'd ask to know
What I was walling in or walling out,
35 And to whom I was like to give offense.
Something there is that doesn't love a wall,
That wants it down.' I could say '**Elves**'[3] to him,
But it's not elves exactly, and I'd rather
He said it for himself. I see him there
40 Bringing a stone grasped firmly by the top
In each hand, like an old-stone savage armed.
He moves in darkness as it seems to me
Not of woods only and the shade of trees.
He will not go behind his father's saying,
45 And he likes having thought of it so well
He says again, "Good fences make good neighbors."

Check Your Comprehension

1. What is the narrator's relationship with his neighbor?

2. What does the first line of the poem mean?

3. What does the line "He is all pine and I am apple orchard" mean?

4. Why does the narrator say "I could say 'Elves' to him"?

5. What is the main idea of this poem?

[2]a spell = a magic trick
[3]elves = small, imaginary human-like creatures

READING

Find out more about **paraphrasing** by looking under **summarizing** in the Reference Guide to Reading Strategies on pages xii–xiv.

Paraphrasing

When a reading is difficult, as poetry sometimes is, it can help to paraphrase, or put phrases into your own words. Paraphrase the poem into prose, that is as if you were telling a story. Paraphrase each of the parts below. The first one is done for you. (This is difficult! It may help to work with a partner.)

1. Something there is that doesn't love a wall,
   That sends the frozen-ground-swell under it,
   And spills the upper boulders in the sun,
   And makes gaps even two can pass abreast.

   Something in nature doesn't love a wall. The frozen ground grows

   under it, and makes the wall break, creating holes so wide that two

   people can walk through them at the same time.

2. The work of hunters is another thing:
   I have come after them and made repair
   Where they have left not one stone on a stone,
   But they would have the rabbit out of hiding,
   To please the yelping dogs.

   _____

   _____

   _____

3. The gaps I mean
   No one has seen them made or heard them made,
   But at spring mending-time we find them there.

   _____

   _____

   _____

4. I let my neighbor know beyond the hill;
   And on a day we meet to walk the line
   And set the wall between us once again.

   _____

   _____

   _____

5. We keep the wall between us as we go.
To each the boulders that have fallen to each.

_____

_____

_____

6. And some are loaves and some so nearly balls
We have to use a spell to make them balance:
'Stay where you are until our backs are turned!'
We wear our fingers rough with handling them.

_____

_____

_____

7. Oh, just another kind of out-door game,
One on a side. It comes to little more:
There where it is we do not need the wall:
He is all pine and I am apple orchard.

_____

_____

_____

8. My apple trees will never get across
And eat the cones under his pines, I tell him.
He only says, 'Good fences make good neighbors'.

_____

_____

_____

9. Spring is the mischief in me, and I wonder
If I could put a notion in his head:
'Why do they make good neighbors? Isn't it
Where there are cows?
But here there are no cows.

_____

_____

_____

10. Before I built a wall I'd ask to know
What I was walling in or walling out,
And to whom I was like to give offense.

_____

_____

_____

11. Something there is that doesn't love a wall,
That wants it down.' I could say 'Elves' to him,
But it's not elves exactly, and I'd rather
He said it for himself.

_____

_____

_____

12. I see him there
Bringing a stone grasped firmly by the top
In each hand, like an old-stone savage armed.
He moves in darkness as it seems to me
Not of woods only and the shade of trees.

_____

_____

_____

13. He will not go behind his father's saying,
And he likes having thought of it so well
He says again, "Good fences make good neighbors."

_____

_____

_____

THINK ABOUT IT

1. Why do you think this poem is called "Mending Wall"?

2. Did you enjoy this poem? Why or why not?

3. Are fences common in your country? What do you think of the practice of building fences?

PART TWO

Families: Father Dearest

Fathers play an important role in every culture. In American culture, their roles are changing. In the past, they were the family members who earned money by working while mothers stayed home with the children. However, in today's changing world, mothers work, fathers sometimes stay home, and relationships are different.

Before You Read

In the following reading, the author talks about her father's habit of worrying.

Before you read, think about these questions:
- Were your parents worriers? What did they worry about?
- What kind of things did your parents warn you about?

Cultural Cues   *Heimlich maneuver* A first-aid technique used when someone is choking.

mini-blinds A type of window covering made of slats of plastic or wood that you can open or close to let in light.

VIGILANCE

BY MEG CIMINO

My father and I were watching a videotape in which my two-year-old nephew, Cameron, ran into view with a spoon sticking out of his mouth. I knew exactly what Dad was going to
5 say; I practically mouthed the words along with him: "He'll trip, and that spoon will go right into his throat." In the next scene Cameron raced around the coffee table. "He's going to split his head open on that table," my father
10 said with alarm. "They should pad the corners."

"I know," I replied. "I can't believe they decided to have furniture!"

Dad smiled, as accustomed to my **mocking**[1] his cautions as I am to hearing his warnings
15 about even the most **mundane**[2] hazards. If my father could, he would pad all the sharp corners in the world.

Like most parents, he has always tried to protect his children. And as a doctor who spe-
20 cializes in public-health issues, he is especially conscious of the seemingly innocuous dangers surrounding us.

I remember stuffing raw cookie dough into my mouth at a friend's house once and being
25 surprised that nobody said a word about **sal-**

monella[3] poisoning. At home, "Are you choking?" was uttered as often as "Did you wash your hands?" The **Heimlich maneuver** was a highly valued skill.

30 Restaurants, Dad warned, presented **myriad**[4] risks, from careless waiters who might drop hot coffee onto your head to employees who didn't wash their hands. If we **scoffed**[5], he would cite examples from his days as New
35 York City's commissioner of health.

Fashion, too, could be dangerous. A few years ago he **confiscated**[6] my coat because I hadn't had it hemmed sufficiently. Sometimes I asked about it, as I might about an **eccentric**[7]
40 family member **banished**[8] to live in the attic. Dad will put on the coat to demonstrate how serious a problem it is.

"Look—it's too long even on me. And this material is so heavy, it would pull you down."
45 "I have never heard of anyone being injured by too heavy a coat."

[3]salmonella = a type of bacteria that causes food poisoning
[4]myriad = many and different
[5]scoffed = mocked, ridiculed
[6]confiscated = took away
[7]eccentric = odd, peculiar
[8]banished = sent away

[1]mocking = making fun of
[2]mundane = boring, usual

"Do you want to be the first? Just cut it off here," he'd say, drawing his hand across his knees.

50   The weather was only one of the many natural menaces from which we had to guard ourselves. To this day, when I walk within yards of tree branches, I blink as I hear his voice: "Watch your eyes!"

55   Of course, as children, we did not always listen to Dad. We had our broken bones, near chokings, electric shocks, car accidents, and illnesses, some of which might have been avoided if we had heeded his advice and not
60 jumped from the tops of slides, run around while eating, yanked the plug while the vacuum cleaner was on, driven too fast and kissed dogs.

When my brothers and sisters and I **reminisce**[9] these days, we recall Dad's telling us
65 not to jump on the trampoline in gym class, because of the possibility of spinal injury, and the driving directions he devised to minimize left turns. Now we find ourselves uttering similar **admonitions**[10]. We phone my brother to
70 tell him that we read about someone dying from the same allergy he has or my sister to warn her about the high lead content of certain **mini-blinds**.

And now Dad has a new generation to
75 guide. His grandchildren have caught on quickly, knowing to wag their fingers and say "That's dangerous!" at the sight of cleaning fluid. "That's too big a bite—you'll choke," three-year-old Margaret tells her two-year-old
80 cousin at a holiday dinner table. As everyone is leaving, we all laugh when my niece bids Dad good-bye: "Be careful, Poppa!"

After a weekend visit to my parents, I have my father drop me off at the quiet suburban
85 train station for my trip back to Manhattan. As I wait, I can see his car in the parking lot; I know that he is watching to see that I board safely, without falling into the space between the platform and the train. Sometimes he parks
90 the car, steps out and walks up the stairs to the opposite platform. We wave at each other across the tracks. He stands there until the train comes and he sees me leave.

When I am seated, I watch him drive off,
95 wanting, as I do more and more often now, to protect him from the world's sharp edges, the way he always tried to protect us. I wish I could give him the reassurance his worrying and caring gave me. As the train pulls away, I whisper,
100 "Be careful, Dad."

[9]reminisce = remember fondly
[10]admonitions = warnings

Source: *Atlantic Monthly*

Check Your Comprehension	**1.** What did the author's father worry about?

2. How did the author feel about her father's warnings when she was younger?

3. Why did the author's father worry about her coat?

4. What things in nature made her father worry?

5. How has the author become like her father?

6. How does she feel about her father's warnings now?

READING

Find out more about **understanding through outlining** by looking in the Reference Guide to Reading Strategies on pages xii–xiv.

Understanding through Outlining

An **outline** gives the main points of an article, and shows the relationship between these parts. Outlining this article can help you to understand the main points. Complete the following outline. Refer to the reading when you need to.

Father's Warnings

1. Dangers from food

    a. _____

    b. _____

    c. _____

    d. _____

2. Dangers from fashion

    a. _____

    b. _____

3. Natural dangers

    a. _____

4. Dangers at school

    a. _____

5. Dangers while driving

    a. _____

VOCABULARY
Adjectives

Look up these adjectives in a dictionary, or discuss them with a classmate. Then, put the correct adjective in the blanks.

mundane   *innocuous*   *raw*

myriad   *eccentric*   *suburban*

1. The neighborhood is _____; it is outside the city.

2. My grandfather is _____; he only wears green shirts and pants, and talks to his rose bushes in Latin!

3. There are _____ dangers in the forest: bears, mosquitoes, and steep cliffs.

4. I prefer to eat _____ vegetables. I like them crunchy!

5. That hike is fairly _____; there are no hills and it's only two miles.

6. The movie was really _____—three hours about the life of a cow!

THINK ABOUT IT

1. Was the author's father a good father, in your opinion?

2. Are you a worrier? What do you worry about?

3. Why do you think the author wrote this essay?

Before You Read

In the following reading, the author talks about her father, whose behavior embarassed her.

Before you read this essay, think about the following questions:
- Is anyone in your family odd in some way?
- Were you embarrassed by your parents when you were a kid?

Cultural Cues

Penn Station A large transportation center in New York City.

Adirondacks A mountain area in New York.

Dinty Moore beef stew A popular brand of canned meat stew.

duct-tape An extremely strong type of tape.

Manhattan A borough of New York City.

Roy Rogers A chain of fast-food restaurants owned by the television cowboy Roy Rogers.

Amtrak The national passenger train system.

northeast corridor The area consisting of Boston, New York, and the roads and railways connecting them.

by Rebecca Barry   DADDY WEIRDEST

My dad just called. He's going to be in the city tonight and wants me to meet him for dinner. Nice, right? Maybe for a child of a normal parent, which I am not. Here's the **scenario**[1]:
5 Dad's traveling on business from upstate New York to Washington, D.C. While a lot of people would just hop on a plane, he will take the evening train from Syracuse, arrive in New York at 10:00 P.M., and check into a sleeper car
10 of the D.C.-bound train, which will leave New York at 5:00 A.M. And if you think that means dinner at a **swanky**[2] late-night **bistro**[3], you're wrong. There's really no place my dad would rather be than **Penn Station.** So if I want to

15 see him, I get to hang out there in the late evening with the heroin addicts until his train pulls in. We'll have chicken sandwiches and a cup of instant hot cocoa at **Roy Rogers,** after which he will kiss me good-bye and go find his
20 sleeping car.

The man loves trains—riding them, photographing them, even listening to them. When I was little, I thought it was normal to take **Amtrak** everywhere; I truly believed that only the
25 filthy rich took domestic flights. I also didn't find it odd that if we had to drive—say, to visit my grandparents—the route was carefully plotted near a railroad track so that somewhere along the way, Dad could stop and take pic-
30 tures.

By the time I reached middle school, I realized that my dad was a freak. By the eighth

[1]scenario = scene

[2]swanky = fancy, high-class

[3]bistro = small restaurant

grade I was the only kid who had never been on an airplane. And it got worse. No other parents
35 played albums with titles like "Sounds of Steam," live recordings of steam engines that sent the dog and cats running for cover. Other parents also weren't teased by neighbors and friends about having memorized all the train
40 schedules in the **northeast corridor.** But Dad remained **oblivious**[4] and **blithely**[5] continued to entertain company with his **uncanny**[6] imitation of an oncoming train that made the dog howl. In ninth grade, the coolest girl in my
45 class, Krista Marshall, decided I was her new best friend, and my father almost ruined my life. Hoping to cement the friendship, I invited Krista on a vacation with my family. In my effort to please, I had forgotten that Dad's defi-
50 nition of vacation is different from most people's. Other families go to Disneyland or to the beach or at least get to stay in a motel. But Frank Barry believes in self-sufficiency, so we ended up in a tent in the woods in the **Adiron-**
55 **dacks.** As was our luck with camping trips, it rained from the first night on, which wouldn't have been a problem if my father wasn't such a fix-it-yourself type of guy and hadn't **duct-taped** our old canvas tent together. But he is,
60 and he had, and the tent leaked. After four days of waking up sopping wet, going for 5- to 10-mile hikes (on which we saw lots of endangered plants but not one cute boy) and living off **Dinty Moore beef stew,** we finally piled
65 back into the car for the four-hour drive home.

Poor Krista, bug-bitten and sneezing, could no longer contain herself when my father pulled off the road in what seemed like the middle of nowhere, got out of the car, and dis-
70 appeared into the woods.

"Why are we stopping?" she asked, a note of panic rising in her voice, probably fearing that we were going to set up camp again.

My mother smiled as if everything and
75 everyone were normal, and said, ""Frank is just going to take some pictures." To my horror, there was my dad, some 20 feet above the ground, leaning out precariously from a railroad bridge to get just the right angle to photo-
80 graph the train when it came along. The train was late and we ended up waiting in the car for 45 minutes. Krista tried not to cry, and I miserably wondered how a man who didn't look **malevolent**[7] could single-handedly de-
85 stroy his own flesh and blood's chances at ever being hip.

I have to admit that my father never really ruined my life. It turned out that Krista's parents have a piece of paper strategically placed
90 over a hole in their living room that says in bold red letters, "What in the hell are you looking up here for?!" Krista always tried to remove it before friends or boyfriends came over, but somehow it always reappeared in all its defen-
95 sive glory. With our socially challenged **progenitors**[8] in common, we became and remain great friends.

I also admit that when not humiliated by my dad's bizarre behavior, I have to love and
100 admire that he's a free spirit. The truth is, he simply doesn't wonder about what other people think. How many other girls have a dad who hitchhiked all over Latin America to photograph trains his first year out of college? Or
105 whose spare time is devoted to the worthy cause of educating the world about the environmental correctness of taking the train? He's a **maverick**[9]. That's cool because I'm kind of like that, too. I don't care if my socks don't
110 match, or if people laugh at me because I obstinately believe that life should be fair. Maybe I got it from him, but I definitely make my own choices, regardless of other people's opinions.

So I guess it's better to have an embar-

---

[4]oblivious = ignorant, not knowing

[5]blithely = happily, freely

[6]uncanny = very realistic

[7]malevolent = evil

[8]progenitors = fathers

[9]maverick = pioneer, free spirit

115 rassing father than one who is busy trying to impress other people. Sometimes I even love my dad all the more for his **quirkiness**[10], like his love for Penn Station. And at least now I have some ammunition when he starts to scold 120 me about being careful in **Manhattan.** I mean, I appreciate his concern and everything, but he's the one sleeping in the train station, not me.

[10]quirkiness = oddness, unusual nature

Source: *Chicken Soup for the Teen Age Soul*

Check Your Comprehension

1. How is the author's father different from most other fathers?
2. What did the author's father do when he got out of college?
3. What kinds of activities did the author find odd when she was a child?
4. Why did the author's family go camping instead of on a more "normal" vacation, like Disneyland?
5. Why did the author feel a close friendship with her neighbor, Krista?
6. In what way were Krista's parents odd, too? Why is this important to the writer?
7. How is the author like her father?
8. How does the author feel about her father now?

READING

Find out more about **finding and understanding the main idea** by looking in the Reference Guide to Reading Strategies on pages xii–xiv.

Finding and Understanding the Main Idea

What is the main point of this article? Select one of the statements below.

_____ 1. The author's father was strange when she was younger, and she hopes that fathers who read this won't be like her father.

_____ 2. She is still humiliated by her father's behavior, and wants to write about it.

_____ 3. Although she thought her father was odd when she was younger, the author appreciates his personality now.

_____ 4. She wanted to write about her experiences with her best friend, Krista.

Now, explain why you chose that one. Find quotations or passages in the reading to support your opinion.

_____

_____

_____

_____

_____

VOCABULARY
Prepositions and New Words

Look at the following pairs of sentences. Fill in the blank in the first sentence of each pair with a word from the preposition list. Fill in the blank in the second sentence with a word from the vocabulary list.

Prepositions	Vocabulary Words
in	*hang out*
on	*bistro*
for	*swanky*
at	*oblivious*

1. My father will be _____in_____ the city tonight. We'll have dinner

   at a ____swanky____ restaurant.

2. Tomorrow, I'll hop _____ a plane to Mexico. I want
   to _____ at the beach there for a while.

3. The noise was so loud it sent me running _____ cover. But
   my friend just walked along _____ to the noise, as if she
   had not heard it.

4. The train pulled in _____ 10:00 P.M. Then we went to a
   small _____ for a late dinner.

THINK ABOUT IT

1. Why do you think the author wrote this article?

2. The author says, "it's better to have an embarrassing father than one who is busy trying to impress other people." Do you agree? Why?

3. Why do you think the author changed her mind about her father?

S Y N T H E S I S

Discussion and Debate

1. How do friendships and family relationships differ?

2. There is a saying, "Blood is thicker than water." What do you think this means? Do you agree with the saying?

3. What is your definition of a family? Is it just blood relatives?

4. Think of another question to ask your classmates about the ideas in this chapter.

Writing Topics

1. In your journal, write about your family. Explain who they are and what they are like.

2. Write a letter to a family member about a new friend you've made. Explain who this person is, and why he or she is important.

3. Choose one family member who you think is unique. Write an essay about this family member. Your essay should talk about how this person has affected you.

4. Imagine you are an advice columnist. Look at the following letter. Write a reply to the writer.

> Dear Aunt Advice:
>
> My mother is driving me crazy! She wants to know everything I do. She makes me come home by ten o'clock, and wants to meet all of my friends before I go anywhere. She won't let me go to movies that have violence or swearing in them. And, I can't date, even though I'm already 14! What am I going to do?
>
> Help me,
> Crazy in Seattle

On Your Own

1. Find an article about communication between men and women. Read it and report on it to your class.

2. Look at the advice column in a newspaper for several days. Look for letters that people write about family problems or difficulties with friends. What kinds of problems do people write about? What kinds of answers does the columnist give?

3. Watch at least one television show about family life. What kind of father does the show portray? Compare your answers to your classmates' answers.

★★★

A L M A N A C   For additional cultural information, refer to the Almanac on pages 217–228. The Almanac contains lists of useful facts, maps, and other information to enhance your learning.

★★★

CHAPTER 5

Geography

The United States has a diverse population, and its land is diverse as well. From rain forests in the Northwest to desert in the Southwest, from the coldest mountains in the Northeast to the warmest islands in the Southeast, the land is like the people: different wherever you go.

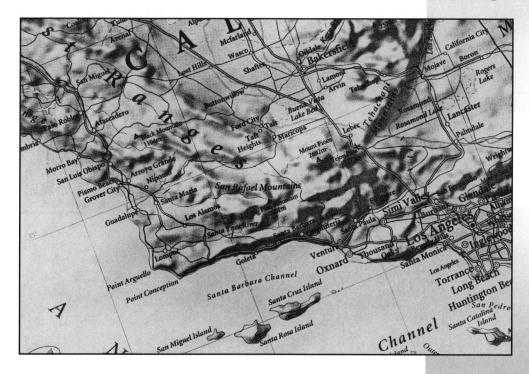

PART ONE
States of Mind

The fifty United States might seem like 50 simple political divisions, but the reality of the situation is much more interesting. Each state has its own unique history and character. Although some states resemble each other, each one has its own story to tell.

Before You Read

Facts About California

Nickname: The Golden State

Population: 31,589,153 (the largest population in the U.S.)

Population Distribution:*
    69 percent European-American
    25.8 percent Hispanic-American
    9.6 percent Asian-American
    7.4 percent African-American

Size: 163,707 square miles (the third largest state in the U.S.)

Entered the Union: September 9, 1850, the 31st State

First European Explorer: Juan Cabrillo, 1542

First European Settlement: 1769, near San Diego

Capital City: Sacramento

Largest City: Los Angeles

State Motto: Eureka! (I found it!)

*does not equal 100 percent, because some people are in more than one category

In this reading, the author discusses the history of the Chinese in California, and the origin of California's nickname, Gold Mountain.

Before you read, think about the following questions:

• Have you visited California? If so, what did you see?

• What do you think the nickname "Forty-Niners" means?

• What do you know about California?

Cultural Cues	***American River*** A river in northern California.
	Sierra Nevada Mountains A large mountain range in northern California. Lake Tahoe is found in the Sierra Nevada.

About the Author	Ronald Takaki is Professor of Ethnic Studies at the University of California, Berkeley. He is the grandson of Japanese immigrants. He is the author of *Strangers from a Different Shore*, and other books about Asians in America.

Searching for Gold Mountain
by Ronald Takaki

One summer day in the 1850s, a traveler in the **Sierra Nevada mountains** of California came upon an interesting sight. In the harsh landscape of tumbled brown rocks he saw "long files of Chinamen working alone." The traveler enjoyed seeing the Chinese men; they broke up "the **monotony**[1] of
5 the landscape." They wore blue cotton shirts, wide-legged trousers, wooden shoes, and broad-brimmed straw hats. In the Chinese fashion of the time, their jet-black hair was cut short, except in back, where each man wore a long braid called a queue.

The men were busy sifting sand from the beds of mountain streams,
10 rocking it back and forth in shallow pans as the water ran out. Like many other people in California in those years, the Chinese miners were **panning for gold**[2].

Gold had been discovered in 1848 along the **American River** in California, on the property of a man named John Sutter. Although Sutter tried to
15 keep the discovery a secret, word of the fabulous find soon reached San Francisco, and hundreds of people deserted the city to set off for the American River. The news spread to the rest of the United States, and to other parts of the world as well. By January of 1849, 60 ships and thousands of overland travelers were headed for California. The California gold rush had begun.
20 More than 70,000 hopeful adventurers **embarked**[3] for California in 1849 alone. Among these "Forty-Niners" were 325 men from China. More Chinese came the next year, and the next. Like the prospectors who came from the

Watch the CNN video on the California Gold Rush.
Discuss these questions:
1. When was the Gold Rush?
2. During the previous year, how much gold did miners remove?
3. How do you pan for gold?

[1]monotony = boredom, sameness

[2]panning for gold = looking for gold in the water by using a pan

[3]embarked = started out

eastern United States and elsewhere, the Chinese hoped to find a fortune waiting for them in the California hills. A few of them *did* find gold—but
25 all of them found a new world and a new way of life, with challenges, fears, and opportunities that they had not expected.

The exciting news about Gold Mountain spread throughout China, filling people with the desire to join the gold rush. One traveler in China said that if everyone who wanted to go to California had been able to afford it, whole
30 Chinese towns would have been emptied. A popular Chinese saying of the time promised that if a man could not get a thousand dollars in California, he would surely get at least eight hundred. But even with only three hundred dollars he could return to China and become "a big, very big gentleman."

Source: *Journey to Gold Mountain: The Chinese in 19th Century America*

Check Your Comprehension

1. Why was California called Gold Mountain?

2. Describe the Chinese men of the 1850s.

3. Who were the Forty-Niners?

4. Who was John Sutter?

5. Why did the Chinese come to California?

6. What did the new settlers find in addition to gold?

7. What was the Gold Rush's effect on China?

8. How much money did it take to be "a big, very big gentleman" in China during the Gold Rush?

 READING

Find out more about **finding and understanding the main idea** by looking in the Reference Guide to Reading Strategies on pages xii–xiv.

Finding and Understanding the Main Idea

Authors write to express an idea, or sometimes many ideas. What do you think Takaki's main reasons for writing this essay were? Check the possible reasons below. If you check more than one, indicate which you think is the **main idea**.

_____ To show that the Chinese are part of California Gold Rush history.

_____ To tell a little about Gold Rush history.

_____ To show the prejudice against the Chinese in the 1800s.

_____ To discuss a part of California history.

_____ To talk about the thousands of prospectors who got rich in the 1800s.

Think about your choice of main idea. Explain in the following space why you chose that main idea. Then discuss your choices with the class.

I chose _____

_____

_____

_____

_____

VOCABULARY
Understanding from Context

Here are some words from the reading that might have been new to you. Find these words in the reading. Then, without looking them up in the dictionary, from the reading and your understanding of the word, write a definition for each of them. Compare your answers with a classmate's.

1. *afford* _____

2. *braid* _____

3. *desert* _____

4. *landscape* _____

5. *miners* _____

6. *monotony* _____

7. *opportunity* _____

8. *prospector* _____

THINK ABOUT IT

1. Three hundred twenty-five Chinese men were among the original 70,000 Forty-Niners. This is not a large number. Why do you think Takaki writes about it?

2. The fascination with gold goes back centuries. Can you understand this fascination? Do you own any gold jewelry? Would you like to? Why or why not?

3. Takaki says that only a few people found gold. Why do you think so many people continued to come to California in spite of this?

Before You Read

Facts About Florida

Nickname: The Sunshine State

1995 Population: 14,165,570 (the 4th largest population in the U.S.)

Population Distribution:*

83.1 percent European-American
13.6 percent African-American
12.2 percent Hispanic-American

Size: 65,756 square miles (the 22nd largest state in the U.S.)

Entered the Union: March 3, 1845, the 27th State

First European Explorer: Ponce de Leon, 1513

First European Settlement: 1564 on the St. John River

Capital City: Tallahassee

Largest City: Miami

State Motto: In God We Trust

*does not equal 100 percent, because some people are in more than one category

In this reading, the author talks about a popular area of Miami, Florida called South Beach. South Beach is especially popular with models, photographers, and young people who enjoy the sunshine, roller skating, and relaxed atmosphere.

Before you read, think about the following questions:

* Have you ever visited Florida? If so, what did you see?
* What do you know about Florida?
* What does the word *seduction* mean?

Cultural Cues

condo condominium. A type of apartment, or home that you purchase.

flea market An open market where people sell used or cheap goods.

the Weather Channel A television channel that broadcasts only weather forecasts.

Ben-Gay A type of medication that is applied to the skin to soothe sore muscles.

bar mitzvah A celebration for a Jewish boy upon turning thirteen. This ceremony marks his entry into manhood.

Harleys Harley-Davidson motorcyles, the most popular American brand of motorcycle.

Little Havana The Cuban-American neighborhood in Miami.

READING

Find out more about **increasing speed** by looking in the Reference Guide to Reading Strategies on pages xii–xiv.

Increasing Speed

Believe it or not, reading more slowly doesn't always help your understanding. In fact, it can result in understanding *less* of what you read, not more.

One way to read more quickly is by reading *groups* of words, rather than single words. Try to read words that form natural groups, that is, groups that are in the same phrase or clause in a sentence. If you read individual words, you are reading like this:

Jeffrey Lew bought his condo in South Beach five years ago.

Your eyes are pausing eleven times! If you read the same sentence in groups, you'll read like this:

Jeffrey Lew bought his condo in South Beach five years ago.

Here, you're pausing only four times. Can you see why you group these words?

Now, read "South Beach Seduction" as quickly as you can, while still understanding the text. Remember, you don't have to understand every word. Keep your eyes moving and try to see groups of words.

Write the time you begin reading

Starting Time: ___:___

 by Stephen DiLauro **South Beach Seduction**

Jeffrey Lew bought his **condo** in South Beach five years ago. Over the years he repeatedly urged me to visit. Then, this past December, he told me over the phone that he had
5 given up on me. I responded that he should look for me on his doorstep in January and got myself a plane ticket that day.

Jeffrey is a gourmet cook. He whips us up a light dinner my first evening in South Beach.
10 After eating, we go out on the terrace overlook-

ing Española Way to watch the street life. This one block projects off of Washington Avenue directly into Barcelona [Street]. In the narrow space between the **terra-cotta**[1] Spanish-style

15 buildings, people flow by on skates, bikes, feet, bordered by palm trees and overlooked by balconies. Palm trees. I want to run out and hug a palm tree.

A knock on the door summons Jeffrey. I
20 overhear only parts of his side of the conversation: "Sugar? No problem . . . my friend Steve . . . Sure. Great!" He comes back out on the terrace. "Put your shoes on. We're going for coffee. Hurry."

25 So much rush and excitement for coffee? "Don't ask questions," he calls from the kitchen as he scoops together a cup of sugar.

We go to the apartment next door where we meet three young women—Holly, whose
30 apartment it is, Rosa, Jennifer—and Jennifer's 5-year-old daughter, Sage.

Each of the three women gives me an embrace and **busses**[2] my cheek to say hello. (This will take place with nearly every woman Jeffrey
35 introduces me to during my stay.) Holly is obviously a model. Rosa dances at Mango's on Ocean Drive. Jennifer's boyfriend, Tony Garcia, is hosting a **hip-hop and acid jazz**[3] music show they are listening to on the radio as we visit.
40 Jeffrey starts doing an improvised rap on why we park on driveways and drive on parkways. Rosa is **in stitches**[4]. Maybe you had to be there. Anyway, I'm glad to be hanging out with my buddy and his friends, the air filled with the
45 intermingling scents of coffee and **Ben-Gay.** Holly threw her back out at a yoga class earlier in the afternoon.

Back in the apartment Jeffrey asks, "Do you see why I'd rather be down here than in New
50 York? It's like this all the time." I'm starting to get the picture.

We go for a walk and Jeffrey points out some of the hot spots on Ocean Drive. It's a Thursday night and the place is throbbing.
55 Music is pulsing everywhere. People are **swathed**[5] in neon light. The **ubiquitous**[6] sound of spoken Spanish brings home to me that I am in a major Latin American capital. The winter and Pennsylvania seem very far away.

60 It's midnight and the phone is ringing as we enter the apartment. News of another social engagement. Back out and into the car.

The next day is sunny—of course. Jeffrey and I spend the afternoon at the beach. Women
65 are sunbathing topless and the ocean is a defining and irresistible blue.

Early in the evening one of his girlfriends shows up. Jeffrey tugs on his ear and I go for a walk.

70 I return down Española Way later and see that the girlfriend's car is gone. Jeffrey is up and ready to go. We take a walk along Lincoln Road and smoke cigars. The chic crowd promenades beneath the palms. Jeffrey tells me the
75 first time he saw a palm tree he wanted to make love to it. At midnight he takes me to Tantra, a club on Española that has grass growing on the floor, and he buys me a birthday **cognac**[7]. I'm 48 years old. We run into some
80 of Jeffrey's friends and hang out until 2 A.M.

It's sunny, but windy and too cool for the beach Saturday, my birthday. Jeffrey is apologizing for the weather, saying I arrived in "the dead of winter." I'm in sandals, shorts and
85 T-shirt and just learned from **the Weather Channel** about the two days of snow and ice that hit eastern Pennsylvania. I assure him that the weather is just fine. Jeffrey has a **bar mitzvah** to attend. Then he's planning to meet a girl-
90 friend at her place in Delray. He apologizes for missing my birthday and I wave him off.

The next morning Jeffrey takes me to the Swap Shop **flea market** in Fort Lauderdale.

---

[1]terra-cotta = a type of red clay material

[2]busses = kisses

[3]hip hop, acid jazz = types of music

[4]in stitches = laughing hard

[5]swathed = covered

[6]ubiquitous = existing everywhere

[7]cognac = a type of strong alcoholic drink

"This is part of the South Florida experience," he explains. Hundreds of bikers on **Harleys** and other big machines are in evidence everywhere. The place is **a total hoot**[8].

My first Sunday night in Miami: Holly and Rosa ask us if we want to stroll with them through the Art Deco fair on Ocean Drive. The evening air is perfect. The two women are beautiful. We walk and laugh and talk and **gawk**[9]. Rosa points out the elaborate sand castle sponsored by Mango's Tropical Cafe, her employer. We all agree that it is the best sand castle any of us have ever seen.

Back at the apartment I gush about South Beach. Jeffrey laughs. "You don't know the half of it yet. It's the dead of winter. I can't even take you out on the boat in this weather. Anyway, I'm having a dinner party for you on Friday. You, me and 15 women. That'll open your eyes."

Friday?

Originally I had planned to stay three or four days. I've been here for four days already. Friday is five days off. I ask if he can stand me as a houseguest for that long.

"Sure. I'm having a ball. Don't worry, I'll let you know when you've been here long enough."

The next day on the phone I explain to my wife that I just can't leave yet. She asks me if I'm hanging out with models. I respond with **an emphatic but noncommittal**[10] "Oh, please!"

By Wednesday morning I've decided that Miami Beach is where I want to live. Jeffrey laughs. "You going to move the family down, too?"

Of course, I waver. He laughs again. "It won't be quite the same experience with your wife and kids here."

That night Howard shows up and the three of us go to Versailles for Cuban food in **Little Havana.** The food is delicious, ample, and surrounded by a kind of glitter that has nothing to do with South Beach. I feel as though I should have had to cross a few international borders to arrive here, but all I had to do was take a ramp off the interstate.

After dinner we walk with our cigars in Coconut Grove. Jeffrey points at me and tells Howard, "He's been walking around with that same grin on his face since he arrived. Look at him."

It's true. I can't stop smiling. For the first time in my life I feel I'm in exactly the right place at exactly the right moment and things can only get better.

Sunday Jeffrey asks me if I have any idea how much longer I'll be staying. I say it seems to me I've been invading his space for an **unconscionably**[11] long time already. "Not at all," he says. "How long have you been here?" He is shocked when I tell him it's been 11 days. "Eleven days! That's amazing. No one has ever lasted that long with me."

Jeffrey assures me again that he loves my company. "But it's time to ease on down the road soon. Shoot for Tuesday."

Tuesday I check into the Clay Hotel two blocks away on Española. On Wednesday, over lunch at the Fernandez Fruit Company on Washington, I explain to Jeffrey that I can't leave yet. If I'm going to move here, there are a few things to check out first.

"What do you mean *if*? It looks to me like you already moved here, neighbor," he laughs.

I'm **pitching**[12] hard on the phone to my wife that night. I tell her we'll live close to the beach. "Is the beach there clean?"

Clean? It's the cleanest beach in the world, I tell her.

"It is not the cleanest beach in the world. Think about what you're saying. Think about some of the beaches we've been to."

I insist that Miami Beach is the cleanest beach in the world.

---

[8]a total hoot = very funny

[9]gawk = stare

[10]emphatic but noncommital = strong but not convincing

[11]unconscionably = immorally, improperly

[12]pitching = trying to convince

"I think it's time for you to come home," she tells me.

175 The next day I tell Jeffrey about the conversation.

"She's right. Remember when you came and I told you I'd let you know when you've been here long enough? You've been here long 180 enough. Go home to your wife."

Soon. Real soon.

Source: *Tropic Magazine*

Ending Time: ___:___

minus starting time ___:___

= number of minutes _____

1,441 ÷ _____ mins. = _____

words per minute

The average native speaker reads 250 words per minute. Keep working on increasing your speed while retaining your understanding.

Check Your Comprehension

1. Who is Jeffrey Lew?

2. Why did the author visit Mr. Lew?

3. What is the author's first impressions of South Beach?

4. What kind of food do the people in the story eat in Miami?

5. What kinds of jobs do Mr. Lew's friends have?

6. What does Mr. DiLauro like about South Beach?

7. What kinds of activities do people do in South Beach, according to the story?

8. How long does Mr. DiLauro stay with his friend? Where does he go next?

9. Why does Mr. DiLauro call his wife?

10. Why do you think the author wrote this story?

VOCABULARY
Phrasal Verbs

This reading contains many phrasal verbs—verbs that include both a main verb and one or two prepositions. Find the phrasal verbs listed below in the reading, and discuss with a partner what they mean. Then complete the following sentences.

Put the correct phrasal verb in the blank, then finish the sentence. Try to use some of the new vocabulary from the reading. You may use the new vocabulary words listed below, or use others that you learned from the chapter. Remember you may need to change the verb forms or other words to fit the meaning of the sentence.

Phrasal verbs: *check out, show up, point out, run into, hang out with, whip up*

New vocabulary: *flea market, gawk, a total hoot, palms, cognac, hip hop*

1. He _pointed out_ the new building to me; it _was surrounded by palms._

2. She _____ at the party dressed in _____
   _____

3. By chance, I _____ my best friend yesterday; he _____

4. My mother _____ a wonderful meal last night; we had _____

5. Have you _____ the new club yet? They have the latest _____

6. I like to _____ with a group of my friends at the mall. It's _____

THINK ABOUT IT

1. Have you ever visited a place that excited you like South Beach excited the author? Where was it? How did you feel there?

2. People often feel more excited about places they visit on vacation than the places they live. Why do you think this is?

3. How does this story show the multicultural history of the United States?

PART TWO

RURAL AREAS: FARM LIFE

In America's past, most people lived in rural areas or on farms. Today, most people live in cities. However, rural life is still a part of the American national character.

Before You Read

Percentage of People Who Work on Farms, 1860–1998

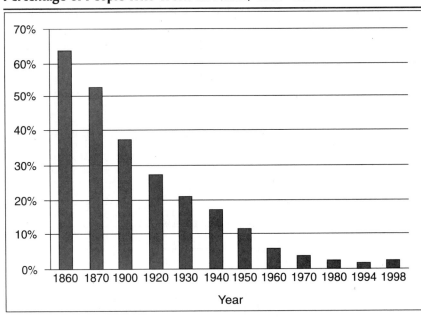

Source: U.S. Dept. of Agriculture

In the following reading, the author talks about some types of farming arrangements that were common at one time in U.S. history.

Before you read, think about the following questions:

- Have you ever visited a farm?
- Are any members of your family farmers?
- Do they own their own farms for work on someone else's farm?

Cultural Cues

tenant farming A system of agriculture in which the workers do not own the land they work. Instead, they pay rent for the land or give a large portion of their crops to the owner.

Civil War A war between the northern and southern states which lasted from 1861 to 1865.

plantation A very large farm on which cotton and tobacco are grown.

Tenant Farming: Not Really a Solution

Before the **Civil War,** the economy of the American South was largely dependent on the labor of **enslaved**[1] Africans. The main products of this region were tobacco and cotton, both of which were **labor-intensive**[2] crops requiring a great many field workers. Near the end of the Civil War, in 1864, the slaves were given their independence.

5　　But the struggle was not over for either the **plantation** owners or for the freed workers. The **former**[3] slaves wanted to get as far away from slavery as possible and to make sure that the freedom they now enjoyed would continue. They also wanted to be able to build successful new lives for themselves as independent citizens of the United States. So these former

10　slaves worked very hard to eliminate any arrangement that resembled the old slave-owner setup. For example, they insisted on moving out of their former slave quarters on the plantation, refused to work under the watchful eye of an **overseer,**[4] would not work under a **gang labor**[5] system, and struggled hard during nonworking hours to achieve social **autonomy.**[6]

15　The plantation owners, on the other hand, were left with the land, seeds, mules and other items needed to grow crops, but with no **labor force**[7] to farm the land. In order to keep former slaves as much-needed laborers, many landowners developed two systems of tenant farming. Through the first type of arrangement, former slaves (and some whites who didn't own

20　land), would pay to rent a piece of land from a farm owner. These renters were called "cash rent" tenants. However, most freed slaves had never had any income and it was impossible for most of them to make enough money to pay rent to a landowner. Therefore, a second type of tenant farming arrangement was developed. This was called the sharecropping system.

25　Through this system the laborer who worked a piece of land "shared" in whatever crops he could **harvest**[8] from the land. In most cases two-thirds to three-quarters of the crop went to the landowner, and only a third to a quarter went to the worker.

　　This system worked all right for a few lucky tenant farmers. Usually,

[1]enslaved = forced to work without pay

[2]labor-intensive = requiring many workers

[3]former = in the past

[4]overseer = manager

[5]gang labor = large group supervised by a single overseer

[6]autonomy = independence

[7]labor force = people who work in a certain industry

[8]harvest = cutting and gathering of crops

30 however, tenants' income from the crops was not large enough to allow them to survive all year round. In response, some landowners set up **commissaries**[9] on their farms or plantations and sold food and other goods to the tenants on a credit basis, allowing them to pay for the items they needed later. Because of this arrangement, many tenants were kept constantly **in**
35 **debt**[10] to their landlord, who in many cases was a former slave owner. Although slavery had been **abolished,**[11] and the former slaves were free, the new arrangement was often not a great deal different form the old one. The dream of true independence had not yet been realized.

It took a long time for the tenant farming system to die out. In fact, in
40 some places things seemed to move in the opposite direction for a while. In the state of Louisiana in the 1860s, more farmland was owned and operated by small landowners than by large landowners. By 1900, however, **absentee owners**[12] and overseer management dominated the agriculture in that state.

40 Aiding in the former slaves' transition toward full independence and the same legal rights as whites, were the many **grass-roots**[13] institutions which they established. Under slavery, most black people had not been allowed to receive an education or establish their own churches. But after the Civil War, unwilling to be second-class citizens in all-white institutions, many
45 blacks helped start small rural churches, neighborhood schools, and even teacher training schools all over the South. Soon African Americans began to back even larger institutions, including **Tuskegee University,** which was founded by Booker T. Washington in 1881 as a school for black students. Tuskegee went on to become one of the most respected universities in the
50 country.

Today, the old tenant farming system has disappeared almost completely and jobs in manufacturing and service industries offer new employment opportunities to millions. Many African Americans now hold high-ranking positions in education, government, and industry. Although tenant farming
55 and sharecropping were one of the only viable opportunities for African Americans to support themselves following the Civil War, in the long run, education, demand for social change, and a great deal of personal determination have been responsible for the tremendous progress made by the descendants of former slaves in the past 100 years.

[9]commissaries = stores owned by the landowner

[10]in debt = owing money

[11]abolished = ended

[12]absentee owners = people who own land but don't live on it

[13]grass-roots = started and operated by a local group

Check Your Comprehension

1. When were enslaved Africans given their freedom?

2. What did the former slaves want to do?

3. What did they want to avoid?

4. What did the plantation owners need?

5. What system developed at this time?

6. Why didn't tenant farming help most freed slaves?

7. What did former slaves do to help insure their continued independence?

8. Who was Booker T. Washington?

 **READING**

Find out more about **understanding definitions** by looking in the Reference Guide to Reading Strategies on pages xii–xiv.

Understanding Definitions

In telling about life after the Civil War, the author defines some facts and terms. Look at the reading again and answer the following questions in your own words.

1. According to the author, what is a *plantation*?

_____

_____

_____

2. What does an *overseer* do?

_____

_____

_____

3. What is a *commissary*?

_____

_____

_____

4. What was *sharecropping*?

_____

_____

_____

VOCABULARY
Learning from Context

The following words might be new to you. Find them in the reading, and without looking in your dictionary, try to understand what they mean. write a short definition for each of them.

1. *region*

_____

2. *independent*

_____

3. *resembled*

_____

4. *crops*

_____

5. *in debt*

_____

6. *former*

_____

THINK ABOUT IT

1. Why do you think that the system of slavery developed in the United States when it did not exist in Europe at the time?

2. What things changed for the slaves after they were freed, and what things stayed the same?

3. Why do you think the freed former slaves did not return to Africa?

Before You Read

The following reading talks about the role of women in managing a farm.

Before you read, think about the following questions:

- Do you think you would enjoy farming (or if you have farmed, did you enjoy it)?
- Do you think a life of farming would be difficult? Why?
- What do you think about women being farmers?

Cultural Cues

Martha Washington The wife of George Washington, the first President of the United States.

Great Depression The economic crisis that began with the fall of the stock market in 1929 and continued throughout the 1930s.

Revolutionary War The fight for independence from England, 1775–1781.

Gone with the Wind A popular novel and movie about the Civil War.

Dakota Territory Land in the central northern part of the United States, which later became states.

Spartan From the Greek city Sparta, which in history was known for a famous war.

the War between the States The American Civil War.

Farm Journal editorial — The Ties That Bind

The farm wife's sense of duty to her family and the land was **forged**[1] by wars. It was **chiseled**[2] and defined as easterners and immigrants broke the sod. It was battered by the 5 **Great Depression.** Families who survived all that searched for meaning in their lives and financial security.

It may have originated with **Martha Washington,** whose commitment to her husband 10 and the 4,000-acre farm at Mount Vernon was as strong as her patriotism to the cause of the **Revolutionary War.** Historians describe Martha as an equal with her husband in the ways of management: George rose at 4 A.M., filling 15 diaries with accounts of his farming; she gave household orders before breakfast, securing time for gardening, the care of her children and training of slaves and servants. **Symptomatic**[3]

of the central tragedy of this nation, Martha's 20 **dowry**[4] included 150 slaves.

In times of war, she talked like a **Spartan** mother to her son going to battle, writes historian Ann Wharton. "I hope you will all stand firm—I know George will," Martha said. With 25 such courageous words on her lips, Martha's sense of duty allowed her to watch George set forth upon his commission—hazardous in the extreme, but if successful, **procuring**[5] the future of their farm, and farms of all Americans.

30 Literature borrows heavily from history. From Martha's real role in the Revolutionary War, the nation's history marches onward, to **the War Between the States.** For the South, it was in part a war to protect a way of life, a 35 **pervasive**[6] part of which was plantation agriculture.

[1]forged = created

[2]chiseled = carved like stone

[3]symptomatic of = characterizing, describing

[4]dowry = in older times, money and property owned by a woman when she was married, usually offered by her family

[5]procuring = getting

[6]pervasive = common

In the beginning of Margaret Mitchell's ***Gone with the Wind***, Gerald O'Hara says to his beautiful, **headstrong**[7] daughter: "Do you
40 stand there, Scarlett O'Hara, and tell me that Tara—that land—doesn't amount to anything?"

Scarlett nodded **obstinately**[8]. But her father pressed on with the central lesson of farming. "Land is the only thing in the world that
45 amounts to anything . . . For 'tis the only thing in this world that lasts. . . . 'Tis the only thing worth working for, worth fighting for—worth dying for."

Scarlett comes to value land as the one
50 good thing amid the war. When her mother is killed, her father goes crazy and the man she loves leaves for battle, Scarlett accepts the responsibilities of running the farm herself.

After the Civil War was over, the nation
55 moved forward to become an industrial and agricultural powerhouse. President Lincoln had initiated the Homestead Act. Land was given to eastern farmers responding to the call, "Go West, young man." So powerful a call, it
60 even **resonated**[9] across the Atlantic to immigrants from northern and central Europe.

Women did not always hear the call, but heard the biblical voice of Ruth: "Whither thou goest, I will go." In O.E. Rolvaag's *Giants of*
65 *the Earth*, a Norwegian farmer brings his wife, Beret, across America to settle in the **Dakota Territory.** Beret attempts to accept her fate as a farm wife on the lonely land. But each day is a battle between her will and the dangerous
70 Dakota winter: "This formless prairie had not heart that beat, no waves that sang, no soul that could be touched. . . . The days wore on; bleak, gloomy days, with cold that congealed all life. . . . But that he could not understand
75 it—that he could not fathom the source of her trouble; seemed **wholly**[10] incomprehensible to her. Didn't he realize she could never be like him? . . ."

Eventually, men and women realized they
80 could never dominate the vast American prairie and plains. But they came to terms with it. As the men **tilled**[11] the land, the women organized the schools and churches to "civilize" the wilderness.

85 Laura Ingalls fell in love with the prairie, becoming a spokesperson for farm life through her newspaper columns and *Little House* book series. When Laura married Almanzo Wilder, the couple lived in town until they could afford
90 a farm. Laura contributed to the family's income by renting rooms and cooking meals for railroad workers.

As land went for sale, the Wilders stretched their resources to buy Rocky Ridge farm. An
95 "ideal home should be made by a man and a woman together," Laura said. She was her husband's partner in farm work, her specialty being the henhouse. She tried to net $1 in profit per hen.

100 The farm economy soared during World War I and, as export markets shriveled, crashing in the 1920s. The 1930s brought a double dose of trouble—drought and debt, captured by John Steinbeck in *The Grapes of Wrath.*

105 "Men stood by their fences and looked at the ruined corn, drying fast now, only a little green showing through the film of dust. The men were silent and they did not move often. And the women came out of the houses to
110 stand beside their men—to feel whether this time the men would break. The women studied the men's faces secretly, for the corn could go, as long as something else remained."

As the Tom Joad family searched field to
115 field for work, the men and children looked to Ma for guidance. "She seemed to know that if she swayed the family shook, and if she ever really deeply wavered or despaired the family would fall, the family will to function would
120 be gone."

---

[7]headstrong = stubborn
[8]obstinately = stubbornly
[9]resonated = echoed, sounded
[10]wholly = completely

[11]tilled = plowed

The Joads went West. Those who stayed behind enlarged their farms. Many sons died in World War II. But in some cases, war survivors brought home brides from Europe and settled 125 into farm life. In *The Bridges of Madison County* by Robert Waller, war bride Francesca Johnson, who grew up in Naples, Italy, absorbs the lesson of American farm life. When a photographer begs her to leave her family behind, she 130 embraces responsibility rather than romance.

"Just my leaving, taking away my physical presence, would be hard enough for Richard. That alone might destroy him," Francesca said. "On top of that, and this is even worse, he 135 would live the rest of his life with the whispers of the people here. . . . They would suffer, too. And they would hate me for it." A city woman might have gone.

Check Your Comprehension

1. According to the author, how was the farm wife affected by war?

2. What was Martha Washington like, according to the essay?

3. What movies are mentioned in this essay?

4. What books are mentioned?

5. Who were the Wilders? Summarize their story.

6. Who were the Joads? Summarize their story.

7. What was the Homestead Act?

8. According to the conclusion of the essay, how is a "city woman" different from a "farm wife."

 **READING**

Find out more about **understanding examples** by looking in the Reference Guide to Reading Strategies on pages xii–xiv.

Understanding Examples

This author makes use of **examples** to make the main points about farm wives. Review the article and complete the following outline. The first example is given for you.

1. Origins of farm wife attitudes in war: <u>Martha Washington helps George.</u>

2. Examples from literature:

   a. _____

   b. _____

   c. _____

   d. _____

   e. _____

VOCABULARY
Verbs

Several verbs that might not be familiar to you are in this reading. Show that you understand the meaning of these verbs by completing the following sentences.

1. She **chiseled** _____ .

2. He **secured** _____ .

3. We will **initiate** _____ .

4. They did not **waver** when _____ .

5. The farmer **tilled** _____ .

THINK ABOUT IT

1. Have you seen any of the movies or read any of the books mentioned in this article? Why do you think the author uses so many of them to make the main point?

2. What does the author mean by the phrase, "symptomatic of the central tragedy of this nation, Martha's dowry included 150 slaves"?

3. Why did the author write this article?

S Y N T H E S I S

Discussion and Debate

1. Is there a difference between rural people and urban people? Explain your opinion.

2. What is the life of a farmer like in your country? Describe what it is like for both men and women.

3. How is the attitude of the "farm women" toward farm life in "The Ties that Bind" different from that of the freed slaves? What attitudes do they have in common?

4. Think of another question to ask your classmates about the ideas in this chapter.

Writing Topics

1. Would you like to live on a farm? In your journal, write about your feelings on rural life. If you have lived on a farm, describe what a typical day is like.

2. What state would you like to visit? Write a short essay in which you describe the state you would like to see, and give your reasons for wanting to visit it.

3. There are many organized events that are held to help certain causes. For example, Farm Aid helps farmers who are in danger of losing their farms. What cause interests you? Write a persuasive essay in

which you describe the cause that concerns you, and demonstrate why it is an important cause.

On Your Own

1. Watch one of the films mentioned in this chapter.
Report on it to your class.

2. What is the life of a farmer like in your country?
Describe what it is like for both men and women.

3. Get information on a national park that interests you.
For information, visit a national park web site at: http://www.nationalparks.org/

4. Read *The Bridges of Madison County* or one of the *Little House on the Prairie* books.
Report on your reading to the class.

5. The life of pioneers and farmers is often idealized on television. Have you seen any of these television programs—*Bonanza, Little House on the Prairie,* or *Dr. Quinn, Medicine Woman*? Watch one of these programs.
How does the program reflect the ideas in this chapter?

6. Locate someone who has lived in California or Florida, or worked on a farm. Interview that person about his or her experience.
Tell your class about the interview and what you learned.

A L M A N A C For additional cultural information, refer to the Almanac on pages 217–228. The Almanac contains lists of useful facts, maps, and other information to enhance your learning.

★★★

Language

As a rule, languages define cultures, and the United States is no exception. But what is "language"? This chapter looks at body language, American Sign Language, talk between men and women, and the distinctive language of some African-Americans.

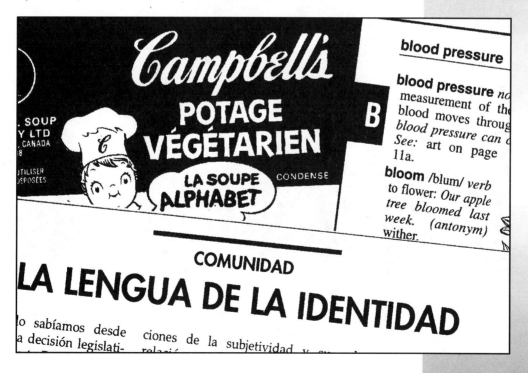

PART ONE

Body Language: THE WINK OF AN EYE

Every culture has gestures—movements or postures that are meaningful. Some of these gestures mean different things in different cultures, while others seem to be universal. America has a rich blend of gestures that are uniquely its own. The deaf culture in America also has a unique language based on hand gestures.

Before You Read

In the following reading, the author explains some common gestures in the United States.

Before you read, think about the following questions:

- What are some common American gestures?

- Are there any gestures that are used in the same way in your culture?

- Which gestures are used in a different way in your culture?

Cultural Cues
> *Martin Van Buren* The eighth president of the United States.
> *Desmond Morris* A scientist who studies human and animal behavior.
> *Charles Darwin* The biologist who promoted the theory of evolution.

About the Author
> Tad Tuleja is the author of over 20 books. He studied cultural history at Yale University, and he studied American popular culture in England.

BY TAD TULEJA

HAND GESTURES

The OK Sign

When the forefinger and the thumb are joined in a circle, the American meaning is approval, a gesture signaling that something is "All right" or "Perfect." The sign has been linked to the expression "OK," as many call it
5 the American OK sign, and take it as a representation of the letter "O." The problem with this interpretation is that only the expression "OK" is native to the United States. ("OK" dates from the 1840s and is probably an abbreviation of **Martin Van Buren's** nickname, Old Kinderhook, a reference to his birthplace in Kinderhook, New York.) The thumb and forefinger sign
10 **predates**[1] Van Buren's presidency by eighteen centuries: the first-century Roman **rhetorician**[2] Quintilian, in his **treatise**[3] on oratory, gives the gesture as a sign of approval.

It's clear, therefore, that the OK sign acquired its modern **connotation**[4] in the ancient world and that the verbal expression was a late, and accidental
15 support. What remains to be explained is the symbolic logic involved. **Desmond Morris** and his colleagues draw a connection between the gesture and the thumb-to-forefinger "precision grip"; such a grip often emphasizes fine points in human conversation. The thumb and forefinger gesture is also among the commonest of *mudras*, or **sacred**[5] finger postures, in the
20 Buddhist and Hindu **contemplative**[6] traditions; as such it appropriately symbolizes the inner perfection that the meditator seeks to achieve. Finally, of course, there is the circle itself, one of the oldest and most common

---

[1]predates = comes before

[2]rhetorician = a person who studies the use of argument in speech or writing

[3]treatise = speech or essay

[4]connotation = shade of meaning

[5]sacred = holy

[6]contemplative = in the act of thinking, concentrating

symbols for perfection in both Eastern and Western cultures. The unspoken message of the ancient sign may be simply, "That is as perfect as a circle."

25 Crossing Your Fingers

We cross our fingers in several situations: when we are wishing for good luck (or wishing to avoid bad luck) and when we are saying something untrue for which we want to avoid being held accountable. The statements that go along with these situations are "Keep your fingers crossed" and "It

30 doesn't count, I had my fingers crossed." These situations have in common the feature of potential danger; thus the gesture serves as protection from bad luck or from the penalties normally associated with lying.

Why should crossed fingers provide protection? Because they are what Desmond Morris and his colleagues call a "cryptic version" of the sign of

35 the cross—a version early Christians could have employed without attracting the attention of pagan eyes. Only after its origins were obscured by long-standing repetition did the twined fingers pattern "come out into the open as a light-hearted social gesture, performed by Christians and non-Christians alike."

40 Shrugging Your Shoulders

Charles Darwin explained the shoulder shrug by the "principle of uncon-scious antithesis." An indignant person, ready to fight for home or honor, holds his head upright, **squares his shoulders**[7], and clenches his fists. A person who feels incapable or uncertain adopts an opposite posture. He

45 hunches his shoulders, tilts his head, and shows his hands palm upward. The message is one of helplessness: "I don't know what to say" or "I couldn't help it." The shoulder shrug has also been defined as a form of defensive **hunching**[8] or symbolic retreat from an unmanageable situation. Raising the shoulders has the apparent effect of lowering the head. The careless half-

50 humorous shrug thus bears a visual **affinity**[9] to the nod or bow of **submis-siveness**[10] and also to a turtle's retraction of its head into its shell. Whether or not our **neurological wiring**[11] is **mimicking**[12] our **reptilian**[13] past here, the meaning of the shrug among humans is the same as that among turtles: "This is too much for me to handle."

[7]square your shoulders = face forward, with the shoulders very straight and even

[8]hunch = a posture where the shoulders are pushed forward and the back rounded

[9]affinity = relationship

[10]submissiveness = letting someone else have power, giving in

[11]neurological wiring = nervous system

[12]mimicking = imitating

[13]reptilian = related to reptiles, such as snakes and lizards

55 **Winking**

As a sign of momentary **collusion**[14] between intimates, winking is common throughout Europe and America. The **implication**[15] of the gesture is that the winker and the winkee share a secret or at least a private understanding of a public situation. Desmond Morris considers the action "directional eye
60 closure." He explains, "Closing the eye suggests that the secret is aimed only at the person being looked at. The other eye is kept open for the rest of the world, who are excluded from the private exchange." An opposite interpretation might also work: The winker keeps one eye on the winkee, while symbolically shutting everyone else out.

Source: *Curious Customs*

Check Your Comprehension

1. What are three different meanings of the "OK" sign?
2. Where did the expression "OK" probably come from?
3. When do Americans "cross their fingers"?
4. How did crossed fingers provide protection in ancient times?
5. What does shrugging your shoulders mean?
6. What does winking mean?
7. What are two different interpretations of why we close only one eye when winking?

READING

Find out more about **understanding by categorizing** by looking in the Reference Guide to Reading Strategies on pages xii–xiv.

Understanding by Categorizing

This reading contains four example of physical gestures used in the United States. Using the chart below, categorize these gestures according to which ones seem to have an historical origin, a religious origin, and an origin in the biology of human behavior. Extend your answer by writing a few words in the appropriate boxes.

	Historical	Religious	Biological
The "OK" sign	Martin Van Buren birthplace— Old Kinderhook	Buddhist finger posture for perfection	
Crossed fingers			
Shrug			
Wink			

[14]collusion = cooperation
[15]implication = meaning

VOCABULARY
Word Parts

Some of the words in this reading may be unfamiliar to you. However, you might recognize the root (shown in boldfaced letters). With a partner, try to think of another word with the same root. One is done for you.

1. re**present**ation   *presently*

2. pre**date**   _____

3. **treat**ise   _____

4. **poten**tial   _____

5. pre**scrip**tion   _____

6. anti**thesis**   _____

7. in**dign**ant   _____

8. re**tract**ion   _____

9. im**plic**ation   _____

10. af**fin**ity   _____

Now, choose five of the words and write sentences using them, showing you understand their meaning.

1. _____

2. _____

3. _____

4. _____

5. _____

THINK ABOUT IT

1. Why do you think so many gestures with ancient origins are still used?

2. Are there any American gestures in this reading that mean something different in your culture?

3. Give some examples of gestures that communicate ideas more powerfully than words. Why do you think gestures have so much power?

Before You Read

In the following article, the authors talk about American Sign Language (ASL) and how it began in the United States.

Before you read, think about the following questions:
- Have you seen someone using sign language?
- Have you ever learned any sign language?

READING

Find out more about **skimming** by looking in the Reference Guide to Reading Strategies on pages xii–xiv.

Skimming

In order to understand the main ideas, read this article once quickly—taking no more than three minutes. Then, write three main ideas you understood from the reading.

1. _____

   _____

2. _____

   _____

3. _____

   _____

Now, reread the article carefully.

Cultural Cues

Martha's Vineyard An island five miles off the southeastern shore of Massachusetts.

ASL IN AMERICA
BY SHERMAN WILCOX AND PHYLLIS WILCOX

A B C D E F G

H I J K L M

N O P Q R S

T U V W X Y Z

American Sign Language (ASL) is the visual/gestural language which is the primary means of communication of deaf people in America and parts of Canada. Current estimates are that between 100,000 and 500,000 people use ASL. This includes native signers who have learned ASL as their first language from deaf parents, hearing children of deaf parents who also learned ASL as their native language, and fluent signers who have learned ASL from deaf people.

The history of ASL is long and rich. Much of its early development, however, remains poorly **documented**[1]. One reason for this is that, like spoken languages, the early forms of signed languages are not preserved. While we can establish the time and circumstances under which education and thus formal instruction in English and various forms of signing, were brought to deaf people in the United States, we have little idea about the structure of the language which deaf people used prior to this. In spite of the **paucity**[2] of information about earlier forms of signed language, we should not doubt that deaf people did communicate with each other in a natural signed language. Even before hearing people began to take an interest in their education, we can be sure that deaf people used a signed language.

We have two sources of evidence that deaf people used a natural signed language before hearing people **intervened**[3]. One is the unique situation which developed on Martha's Vineyard in the late seventeenth century. **Martha's Vineyard** is an island five miles off the southeastern shore of Massachusetts. From 1690 to the mid-twentieth century, a high rate of **genetic**[4] deafness appeared in the island population. Where the normal incidence rate for deafness in the population in nineteenth century America was approximately 1 out of every 5700 people, the incidence on Martha's Vineyard

[1]documented = written about, recorded
[2]paucity = lack, small amount (of something)
[3]intervened = came between things; interfered
[4]genetic = related to the genes, or inherited from family

35 was 1 out of every 155. In some areas of the island the ratios were even
higher; in one town, for example, 1 in every 25 people was born deaf, and
in a certain neighborhood the ratio was as high as one in four.

Martha's Vineyard was an excellent example of a strong and **flourishing**[5]
deaf community. What makes it especially interesting is that there is evidence
40 of an **indigenous**[6] signed language being used on the island. The first deaf
islander, who arrived with his wife and family in 1692, was fluent in some
type of signed language. Many of the families which inhabited the island
moved there from the Boston area; before this, they had immigrated from
a region in England known as the Weald in the county of Kent. Almost all
45 of the deaf inhabitants of Martha's Vineyard could trace their ancestry back
to this small, isolated area in England.

As the deaf community on Martha's Vineyard flourished, so did the
language. We can only **surmise**[7] that this local signed language was based
on a regional variety of British sign language. Soon, it spread in use to the
50 entire island so that almost every individual, deaf and hearing, was able to
use the Vineyard sign language. The impact on deaf people . . . must have
been tremendous. With much of the hearing population of the island bilingual
in spoken English and Vineyard sign language, deafness was not viewed as
55 a handicap. Deaf people were full participants in all aspects of island society.

Source: *Learning to See: Teaching American Sign Language as a Second Language*

Check Your Comprehension

1. Who uses ASL?

2. What is ASL?

3. For how long have people who are deaf been using sign language?

4. What is the importance of Martha's Vineyard in the history of people who are deaf in America?

5. Why is Martha's Vineyard so interesting in the history of ASL?

6. What was the background of the deaf population on Martha's Vineyard?

7. What was the effect of Vineyard sign language on the population?

[5]flourishing = blossoming, growing
[6]indigenous = native
[7]surmise = guess

VOCABULARY
Academic Language

This article uses sophisticated vocabulary and phrases that are characteristic of academic writing.

Look at the following sentences taken from the reading. Rewrite them in your own words. Start by defining the underlined words; then put the phrases together.

1. American Sign Language (ASL) is the visual/gestural language which is the primary means of communication of deaf people in America and parts of Canada.

   Most deaf people in the U.S. and Canada communicate using

   American Sign Language which is a carefully worked out series of

   hand and finger movements.

2. While we can establish the time and circumstances under which education and thus formal instruction in English and various forms of signing, were brought to deaf people in the United States, we have little idea about the structure of the language which deaf people used prior to this.

3. In spite of the paucity of information about earlier forms of signed language, we should not doubt that deaf people did communicate with each other in a natural signed language.

4. Where the normal incidence rate for deafness in the population in nineteenth century America was approximately 1 out of every 5700 people, the incidence on Martha's Vineyard was 1 out of every 155.

5. Many of the families which inhabited the island moved there from the Boston area; before this, they had immigrated from a region in England known as the Weald in the county of Kent.

6. With much of the hearing population of the island <u>bilingual</u> in spoken English and Vineyard sign language, deafness was not viewed as a <u>handicap.</u>

_____

_____

_____

THINK ABOUT IT

1. Would you like to learn sign language? Why or why not?

2. In what ways do you think ASL is similar to verbal language? In what ways do you think it is different?

3. Do you think ASL is just as effective a means of communication as verbal languages? Why or why not?

PART TWO

DIFFERENCES:
NOT SO DIFFERENT AFTER ALL?

Although most Americans speak English, there are differences
in the English they speak. Some of these differences might be
cultural, while others might be more personal.

Before You Read   Look at the survey below. Ask as many men and women as you can these
eight questions. Keep a record of their responses and bring them to class.

	Question	Men's answers	Women's answers
1.	What kind of movies do you like?		
2.	What is your favorite kind of car?		
3.	What is your favorite color?		
4.	How much money would you need in order to consider yourself rich?		
5.	Who is your favorite actor?		
6.	What's your favorite way to spend a free afternoon?		
7.	Do you enjoy shopping?		
8.	How many pairs of shoes do you have?		

The following reading is taken from the very popular book, *Men are from Mars, Women are from Venus*, by John Gray. In this reading, Dr. Gray explains the source of miscommunication between men and women.

Before you read, think about the following questions:

- Do you communicate well with the opposite sex? Why or why not?
- Are there communication problems between the sexes?

Cultural Cues

Martians and Venusians The author's words for men and women, from the title of his book, *Men are from Mars, Women are from Venus*.

READING

Find out more about **active reading** by looking in the Reference Guide to Reading Strategies on pages xii–xiv.

Active Reading

When you read a text, you are more than a passive observer of words. A good reader thinks about what he or she is reading, and has an internal "conversation" with the author.

One way of making this conversation more real is to make notes on the text. Reread the text and make notes in the margin. These can be simple notes: do you agree or disagree with the ideas? Do they make you angry? You may want to use a simple notation system:

Put a **+** by ideas that you agree with

Put a **−** by ideas you disagree with

Put a **!** by ideas that make you angry

Put a ☺ by ideas that you enjoyed reading

As you read this essay, use this marking system. Refer to your notes when you get to the "Think About It" section for discussion.

SPEAKING **DIFFERENT** LANGUAGES
BY JOHN GRAY, PH.D.

When the **Martians and Venusians** first got together, they **encountered**[1] many of the problems with relationships we have today. Because they recognized that they were different, they were able to solve these problems. One of the secrets of their success was good communication.

[1]encountered = met

5   **Ironically**[2], they communicated well because they spoke different languages. When they had problems, they would just go to a translator for assistance. Everyone knew that people from Mars and people from Venus spoke different languages, so when there was a conflict they didn't start judging or fighting but instead pulled out their phrase dictionaries to under-
10 stand each other more fully. If that didn't work they went to a translator for help.

> The **Martian and Venusian** languages had the same words,
> but the way they were used gave different meanings.

You see the Martian and Venusian languages had the same words, but
15 the way they were used gave different meanings. Their expressions were similar, but they had different **connotations**[3] or emotional emphasis. Misinterpreting each other was very easy. So when communication problems emerged, they assumed it was just one of those expected misunderstandings and that with a little assistance they would surely understand each other.
20 They experienced a trust and acceptance that we rarely experience today.

Expressing Feelings Versus Expressing Information

Even today we still need translators. Men and women seldom mean the same things even when they use the same words. For example, when a woman says "I feel like you never listen," she does not expect the word
25 *never* to be taken literally. Using the word *never* is just a way of expressing the frustration she is feeling at the moment. It is not to be taken as if it were factual information.

> To fully express their feelings, women assume poetic license to use
> various superlatives, metaphors, and generalizations.

30
To fully express their feelings, women assume **poetic license**[4] and use various superlatives, metaphors, and generalizations. Men mistakenly take these expressions literally. Because they misunderstand the intended meaning, they commonly react in an unsupportive manner. In the following chart ten complaints easily misinterpreted are listed, as well as how a man might
35 respond unsupportively.

[2]ironically = opposite from what you'd believe

[3]connotations = shades of meanings

[4]poetic license = freedom to exaggerate, or change the facts a little for effect

Ten Common Complaints That Are Easily Misinterpreted

Women say things like this	Men respond like this
"We never go out."	"That's not true. We went out last week."
40 "Everyone ignores me."	"I'm sure some people notice you."
"I am so tired, I can't do anything."	"That's ridiculous. You are not helpless."
"I want to forget everything."	"If you don't like your job, then quit."
45 "The house is always a mess."	"It's not always a mess."
"No one listens to me anymore."	"But I am listening to you right now."
"Nothing is working."	"Are you saying it is my fault?"
"You don't love me anymore."	"Of course I do. That's why I'm here."
50	
"We are always in a hurry."	"We are not. Friday we were relaxed."
"I want more romance."	"Are you saying I am not romantic?"

55   You can see how a "literal" translation of a woman's words could easily mislead a man who is used to using speech as a means of **conveying**[5] only facts and information. We can also see how a man's responses might lead to an argument. Unclear and unloving communication is the biggest problem in relationships. The number one complaint women have in relationships
60 is: "I don't feel heard."
     Even this complaint is misunderstood and misinterpreted!

> The number one complaint women have in relationships is:
> **"I don't feel heard."**
> Even this complaint is misunderstood and misinterpreted!

65   A man's literal translation of "I don't feel heard" leads him to **invalidate**[6] and argue with her feelings. He thinks he has heard her if he can repeat what she has said. A translation of a woman saying "I don't feel heard so that a man could correctly interpret it is: "I feel as though you don't fully understand what I really mean to say or care about how I feel. Would you
70 show me that you are interested in what I have to say?"

[5]conveying = giving
[6]invalidate = not find important

Source: *Men Are from Mars, Women Are From Venus.*

If a man really understood her complaint then he would argue less and be able to respond more positively. When men and women are **on the verge**[7] of arguing, they are generally misunderstanding each other. At such times, it is important to rethink or translate what they have heard.

Check Your Comprehension

1. According to the author, in what way do men misinterpret women?
2. What kinds of speech distinguish women's talk, according to the article?
3. What is the biggest problem in relationships, according to Gray?
4. Does Gray think that men are unsupportive? Why or why not?
5. What does the author mean by, "they communicated well because they spoke different languages"?
6. What is the most common complaint women have in communicating with men?
7. What is the most important problem that men feel in communicating with women?

VOCABULARY
Using New Words

The following words, taken from the reading, might not be familiar to you. Show you understand the words by completing the following sentences.

1. Yesterday, I **encountered** _____ .
2. The fact that I _____ doesn't **invalidate** the experiment.
3. The crowd was **on the verge** of _____ .
4. **Ironically,** _____ .
5. _____ is a **metaphor** for

   _____ .

6. _____ **emerged** recently.

THINK ABOUT IT

1. What do you think of the author's argument? Is it accurate? Does it exaggerate? Review your "Active Reading" notes to help the discussion.
2. What do you think is the biggest problem in relationships between the sexes?
3. What other differences have you noticed in men's and women's styles of communicating? Refer to the survey you did before the reading. How do those observations fit into Gray's argument?

[7]on the verge = at the point, nearly

Before You Read

African-Americans have played important roles in America's history. They have made important inventions and discoveries, created great works of art, and excelled in science, music, medicine, and sports. The U.S. Post Office has issued many stamps to honor the achievements of African-Americans. These are only four of the dozens that have been issued.

Mary McLeod Bethune Co-founder of Cookman-Bethune College, the National Council of Negro Women, and Vice President of the NAACP

Paul Laurence Dunbar A poet and writer; born in Ohio; he was the son of former slaves, he attended public schools, and worked as an elevator operator before becoming a writer.

W.E.B. DuBois A civil rights leader who co-founded the NAACP (National Association for the Advancement of Colored People)

Ralph Bunche First African-American to be a division head in the Department of State, Nobel Prize winner

 Watch the CNN video on African-American language.
Discuss these questions:

1. Why are some people against using Black dialect in the classroom?

2. Why is Black dialect controversial among teachers?

3. According to the report, when is it okay to use Black dialect?

In this article, the author talks about a dialect of English spoken by some African Americans.

Before you read, think about the following questions:

- Have you noticed any differences in American dialects?
- What stereotypes are associated with different dialects?
- Do you think the standard English taught in schools is the only "correct" form of English?

Cultural Cues

Board of Education A group of elected officials who supervise the educational institutions in a community.

Ebonics   One of several terms used to describe a distinct dialect of English used by some members of the African-American community in the United States.

Meet the Press   A television interview program.

Congressional Black Caucus   A group of members of congress who try to pass laws which benefit African-Americans.

Ebonics: A Language Debate

In December of 1996, the Oakland, California **Board of Education** received nationwide attention after declaring, **in essence,**[1] that African-American English, or "Ebonics," is not a **dialect**[2] of American English, but a separate language which has developed from the distinct African American culture
5   in the United States. Although the Board of Education later retreated from this statement, at the time this classification of Ebonics as a separate language led to the development of an Ebonics policy in the public school system. Basically, this policy suggested that, rather than **banishing**[3] African American English from the classroom, it should actually be used as a tool
10   with which to teach standard English.

The Board of Education said, "Too many African American children are entering school year after year speaking differently, and it is **obstructing**[4] their ability to learn. Let's recognize that this is happening." What the board was saying was that students who speak African-American English should
15   not be criticized or **harshly**[5] corrected, but given special assistance in learning **standard English**[6] in much the same way as a student who moved from Mexico and spoke only Spanish would receive training in English as a second language.

Carolyn Getridge, Oakland's school superintendent, said the poor aca
20   demic record of some African American students in the public schools in Oakland means that administrators and teachers there must do something dramatic to try to improve the language skills of these students. Getridge said that having teachers simply tell students that the way they speak is

[1]in essence = in reality, in fact
[2]dialect = a particular variety of a language
[3]banishing = sending away, driving out
[4]obstructing = getting in the way of
[5]harshly = roughly, sharply
[6]standard English = the English taught in grammar books

non-standard, without explanation and without **empathy,**[7] is a terrible mistake. "The students begin to **shut down,**[8]" she said. "We want to change
that reality."

The Ebonics controversy has divided African American leaders. Some
feel that recognizing that some African American students who enter school
do not speak standard English, is the first step toward helping these students
achieve success in school. But other African Americans, including the Rever-
end Jesse L. Jackson, said that movement toward Ebonics would limit
African American students' ability to compete for jobs against graduates
who speak standard English. On NBC's "**Meet the Press,**" Jackson said, "I
understand the attempt to reach out to these children, but this is an unaccept-
able surrender borderlining on **disgrace,**[9]" It's **teaching down**[10] to our
children and it must never happen."

Oakland school officials, joined by Representative Maxine Waters (Democrat of California), who leads the **Congressional Black Caucus, ada-
mantly**[11] defended the Ebonics policy and insisted that it had been
misinterpreted as an attempt to lead students away from standard English.
School officials said they simply want Oakland teachers to devote more
time—and show more sensitivity—to students who rely on African American
English and help them better understand the differences between their
language patterns and standard English.

Part of the confusion stems from the fact that many people involved in
the disagreement did not understand the difference between a language and
a dialect. All languages were originally dialects—ways of speaking developed
by a group of people so that they could communicate with each other. One
reason a dialect becomes a language is that the written and oral forms
provide enough **concrete**[12] examples of its use for someone to make up rules
about it. **Linguists**[13] study these examples and start writing dictionaries and
grammar books that describe how the forms are used. This regularized set
of forms eventually becomes a distinct language.

Linguists refer to the quote, "a language has an army and a navy" to
emphasize the difference between a language and a dialect. In other words,
they say that the dialect that becomes a standard language is the one that
is used by the economic, political, educational, and social leaders of a certain
area. This **prestige**[14] dialect then becomes the standard language of a region
because the most powerful people use it. However, a variety of dialects of
the language continue to exist, and new ones are developing all the time.

---

[7]empathy = emotional understanding

[8]shut down = stop working

[9]disgrace = shame, lack of respect

[10]teaching down = lowering the level of instruction

[11]adamantly = firmly, strongly

[12]concrete = definite, positive

[13]linguists = people who study languages

[14]prestige = respected, influential

Participants on both sides of the Ebonics debate would do well to remember that standard languages are not **sacred entities**[15] and that they come and go over time. Classical Latin was once the most important standard language on the European continent. But with the Roman Empire's loss of
65 economic and political power, Latin died out, and several "sub-standard" dialects of Latin gained strength and eventually **evolved**[16] into standard languages in their own right—among them French, Spanish and Italian. In the same way, what we think of today as "standard" English, is only one of many dialects of English, including Ebonics, some of which may well become
70 standard languages in the future.

Check Your Comprehension

1. What is Ebonics?

2. Why was Jesse Jackson against Ebonics programs in the public school system?

3. What is the difference between a language and a dialect?

4. What happened to Latin?

 **READING**

Find out more about **understanding arguments** by looking in the Reference Guide to Reading Strategies on pages xii–xiv.

Understanding Arguments

What is the main argument in this article? What are the people quoted in the article trying to convince you to believe? How are these ideas supported?
   Fill out the following chart with information from the reading.

Idea	Reason
1. Carolyn Getridge said that students should not be told the way they speak is wrong.	They will shut down and stop learning.
2. Jesse Jackson said that the Ebonics movement would hurt African-American children.	
3. Maxine Waters said that Ebonics would not lead students away from standard English.	
4. A prestige dialect eventually turns into a standard language.	

[15]sacred entities = holy things
[16]evolved = developed naturally and gradually

VOCABULARY
Using New Words

Review the footnotes and the reading. Look up any of these words you don't know. Then match the words that mean the same thing.

1. in essence		**a.**	ability to imagine another person's feelings
2. dialect		**b.**	stop
3. empathy		**c.**	a form of a language
4. shut down		**d.**	having importance
5. linguist		**e.**	getting in the way of
6. prestige		**f.**	person who studies languages
7. teach down		**g.**	really
8. obstructing		**h.**	simplify instruction

Now write sentences using three of the words or phrases in the first column. Be sure your sentences show you understand the meaning of the word.

1. _____

2. _____

3. _____

THINK ABOUT IT

1. Are there dialects in your home country that are not as respected as the standard language or dialect? Who speaks these dialects?

2. Do you agree with the idea of using a person's home language or dialect to help teach them a new language or a new dialect of their language? Why or why not?

3. Have you ever been criticized because of your language? If so, what was your reaction?

SYNTHESIS

Discussion and Debate

1. Swearing is very controversial. Some argue that this language has no place in a "civilized society." Others say it is a natural part of human communication. What do you think?

2. This chapter may present some pessimistic views: men and women have trouble communicating, blacks and whites don't always speak the same language, even body language can have a negative impact. What are your ideas on these issues? What is the positive side to these arguments?

3. Think of another question to ask your classmates about the ideas in this chapter.

Writing Topics

1. In your journal, write about an important language experience you've had. Maybe it was the first time you tried to speak English, or a time when you were successful at giving a speech.

2. Write a paragraph about language in your native language. Then, try to translate that paragraph into English. Finally, write another paragraph about the translation experience. Was it easy? Hard? Did you know the English words for the words in your language?

3. Some people in the United States believe that English should be America's "official" language. Others feel that America's history is rich in language, and different languages should be taught and accepted. What do you think? Write an essay in which you argue for one side or the other. You may want to do some reading about the topic first. Check the newspapers or the Internet for more information.

On Your Own

1. Go to a public place and observe people for a couple of hours. Take notes on their language and gestures. Also make note of their ethnic backgrounds, ages, and genders. What differences do you notice? What do you conclude from your observations?

2. Find a book about sign language. Learn a few signs and demonstrate them for your classmates, signing along with a verbal translation of their meaning.

3. Go to the library or the Internet and research one of the African Americans mentioned on page 127. Make a report to your class about what you learned.

4. Read John Gray's book *Men Are From Mars, Women Are From Venus.* Report on the book to your class.

★★

A L M A N A C For additional cultural information, refer to the Almanac on pages 217–228. The Almanac contains lists of useful facts, maps, and other information to enhance your learning.

★★★

CHAPTER 7

Beliefs

Americans are known for being practical and sensible. This chapter shows us another side of American life, the belief in the unexplained and in the possibility of life in outer space.

PART ONE

The UNexplained

What do Americans believe? What do they believe *in*?
The answers to these questions are as varied as the American population.
This section looks at the work of astrologists and psychics,
two controversial subjects.

Before You Read

Predictions for 1997 and 1998 made by psychics

- Sarah "Fergie" Ferguson, former British royalty, will join the cast of the television program "Melrose Place." In real life, she will marry the clothing designer, Calvin Klein.

- Madonna will become so concerned about the quality of children's television shows she will revive the Mickey Mouse Club, and star in it herself.

- All cats will have to be killed because they will carry a virus that blinds people.

- Doctors will cure the common cold.

- Cuban leader Fidel Castro will be overthrown and move into a Beverly Hills mansion.

- A drink that makes your skin glow bright green in the dark will become popular with nighttime runners and bicyclists.

- Deserts will bloom like gardens after scientists create "walking vegetables" that can move from place to place searching for water.

Cultural Cues

Greek and Babylonian cultures Groups of people living in the Mid East and in western Asia more than two thousand years ago.

talk show A television program in which guests talk with an interviewer in front of a live audience.

Psychic Phenomena: What's Going on Here?

For thousands of years people in various parts of the world have claimed that it is possible for human beings to learn about the future through the

use of **psychic**[1] abilities. The power to do this is sometimes referred to as "the sixth sense." Believers say that this special sense exists alongside the
5   usual five physical senses of seeing, hearing, tasting, smelling and touching. This **faculty**[2] is thought to reveal information not available to the ordinary mind. Over the years, this sixth sense has been given a lot of different names and people have claimed to see evidence of it in a variety of different forms. But all these beliefs have one thing in common: they demonstrate a
10 **conviction**[3] that hidden knowledge can be found, and insight about future events can be gained, by using special abilities of the mind which are not usually used in everyday life.

The records of the early **Greek and Babylonian cultures** contain references to **mediums**[4] and **oracles**[5] who were thought to be able to communi-
15 cate with the gods. Typically, the oracle would go into a dreamlike state called a trance. In this condition, they would contact the gods and then deliver divine messages to the listeners. Other ways of obtaining special **revelations**[6] included the interpretation of dreams and the attempt to make contact with the souls of people who had died. In early Rome, and up until
20 400 **A.D.**,[7] people called augers performed elaborate ceremonies in order to receive guidance from the gods and give advice to the Roman citizens. Other ancient methods of finding guidance include the use of **astrology,**[8] **numerology,**[9] the interpretation of tea leaves, the "reading" of the lines in the palm of the hand, looking into crystal balls for information, and the use
25 of special fortune telling cards. All of these methods are still used with varying degrees of seriousness in various parts of the world today.

Americans have always shown a special interest in psychic **phenomena.**[10] In the late 1880s, the **Spiritualist**[11] movement grew rapidly in the United States, largely due to the well-publicized experiences of two young
30 sisters, Margaret and Kate Fox, who claimed to be able to communicate with spirits "on the other side." At a typical **séance,**[12] those who wished to contact the spirits of dead relatives would sit in a circle around a table in a darkened room holding hands with the sisters. The medium would then call out to the person she was trying to contact and a response might be

---

[1]psychic = supernatural, intuitive

[2]faculty = special ability

[3]conviction = strongly-held belief

[4]mediums = person who communicates with the spirits of the dead

[5]oracles = person or place able to give information about the future

[6]revelations = information, discoveries

[7]A.D. = after the birth of Christ

[8]astrology = using the stars to understand the present and predict the future

[9]numerology = using numbers to gain supernatural understanding

[10]phenomena = events, occurrences

[11]Spritualist = those who believe they can contact the dead

[12]séance = meeting

35 received, sometimes in the form of tapping sounds on the table. Later, Margaret Fox claimed that the events that people observed at her séances were merely tricks. Despite the fact that many reports of psychic phenomena proved to be false, The Society for Psychical Research was founded to examine the claims of spiritualism.

40 One of the most respected groups to undertake research into the field of psychic phenomena is the **Parapsychology**[13] Laboratory at Duke University in North Carolina. A group of researchers at this institution began to apply the **rigorous**[14] methods of scientific research to the study of this field. These researchers used laboratory experiments to study the capacity of the

45 human mind to make use of two abilities: extrasensory perception and psychokenesis. Extrasensory perception (ESP) is the ability to know something that you couldn't possibly know by using the usual five senses. Psychokenesis (PK) is the ability to move an object using only the powers of the mind.

50 Typically, the Duke team conducts mathematically-based studies involving the use of special playing cards and ordinary **dice**.[15] To test a subject's level of ESP, the researcher uses a deck of 25 cards, each of which has a simple design on its face: a star, a circle, a cross, a square, or a series of wavy lines. A laboratory assistant stares with great concentration at the

55 face of each of the 25 cards which the subject is not allowed to see. Then, the subject tells what he or she thinks is pictured on each card. A score of five correct out of 25 is considered pure chance. Scores higher than that are thought to indicate the existence of ESP. To test a subject for psychokenetic abilities, the researcher asks the subject to try to make certain numbers on

60 the dice fall face upward. The researcher then throws dice against a wall and keeps track of how often the dice produce the requested numbers. After correlating the scores on individual ESP tests and PK tests with the scores on thousands of such tests, researchers have concluded that psychic phenomena do indeed exist.

65 In recent years, there has been increased interest in psychic phenomena in the United States. There are currently hundreds of psychic telephone **hotlines**[16] and Internet web sites, and countless books have been published on the subject. These resources will supply the user with advice about current decisions and future events, supposedly based on information ob

70 tained through psychic means. Even police departments have begun to admit to using psychics to help solve difficult cases.

One psychic who has received a lot of attention is Sylvia Browne who lives in Campbell, California. Ms. Browne has appeared on several **talk**

[13]parapsychology = the study of psychic phenomena

[14]rigorous = very serious, strict

[15]dice = cubes with dots on the side used in games of chance

[16]hotlines = phone numbers where someone answers 24 hours a day

75 **shows** where she has discussed and demonstrated her ability to communicate with spirits of the **deceased**.[17] Brown says that she can see both "earthbound ghosts," which look just like living people, and spirits from "the Other Side," which are less clear and sometimes communicate through gestures and pantomime. Ms. Browne's web site states that her goals are: ". . . to prove that the soul survives death, that God is a real and living 80 presence, and that there is a Divine Plan to our lives. . . ."

A psychic reading over the phone with Ms. Brown costs $450. Her web site includes a listing of her upcoming TV appearances, lectures, and predictions for the future. Included in her predictions for the next hundred years are these items:

85 • Electrical cars will have flotation ability for water travel.
• Babies will be birthed in water all the time, with music, incense, and green and lavender lights.
• There will be no U.S. Presidency. Instead, the government will go back to a Greek Senate structure.
90 • By 2055 most people will live in domed cities due to poor atmospheric conditions.

Whether you believe in psychic phenomena or not, it is a subject you will probably be hearing more about. Interest in the sixth sense seems to be increasing, despite out current fascination with technology. In fat, research- 95 ers who specialize in "the new physics" are beginning to agree that there are some things about our world that just can not be accounted for using purely physical explanations. It looks like psychic phenomena are likely to be a subject of just as much fascination in the future as they have been in the past.

Check Your Comprehension

1. What are the five senses?

2. What is the "sixth" sense?

3. How did oracles in Greece and Babylon obtain their information?

4. Who was responsible for early interest in spiritualism in the United States?

5. What is special about the studies being conducted at Duke University?

6. How do people learn about Ms. Browne's work?

---

[17]deceased = no longer living, dead

READING

Find out more about **scanning** by looking in the Reference Guide to Reading Strategies on pages xii–xiv.

Scanning

You may recall that **scanning** is reading through something quickly for specific information. Scan the article and answer the questions below.

1. What were psychics called in Greece and Babylon? _____

   _____

2. What were psychics called in ancient Rome? _____

   _____

3. Name several ancient methods of finding out about the future. _____

   _____

4. When did the Spiritualist movement start in the U.S.? _____

5. Where is Duke University located? _____

6. What items do researchers at Duke use to test for ESP abilities? ____

7. What items do researchers use to test for PK abilities? _____

8. Where does Sylvia Browne live? _____

VOCABULARY
Using New Vocabulary

Complete the following sentences showing that you understand the meaning of the words in **boldface**.

1. If a person is **psychic,** he or she can _____

   _____ .

2. When a person is in a **trance,** he or she _____

   _____ .

3. _____ in _____ **A.D.**

4. **Astrology** involves _____ .

5. People ask for a **séance** so that they can _____

   _____ .

6. _____ is a **rigorous** sport.

7. People sometimes try to use **ESP** to _____ .

8. If a person is **deceased,** he or she _____ .

THINK ABOUT IT

1. Do you believe in any sort of psychic phenomena? Why or why not?

2. Would you ever go to a séance? Why or why not?

3. Do any of Ms. Browne's predictions for the next hundred years make sense to you? Which ones? Why?

Before You Read

Daily Horoscope

Forecast for Monday

Aries: You're still finding your place in the world. It isn't easy making everyone happy! Concentrate on yourself.

Taurus: Your enemies are against you today. They accuse you of many things. Tell the truth, and everything will be okay.

Gemini: You are doing many new things, but this upsets people close to you. Are they concerned about you, or about themselves?

Cancer: Everyone is telling you what to do, but you should keep doing your job. You'll accomplish the things you want if you don't listen to them.

Leo: You will surprise yourself today. You have been telling yourself that you can't do the things you want. Today, you can!

Virgo: Listen to yourself today. Someone is trying to upset you. Be true to yourself.

Libra: You need your enemy's support. Avoiding the problems won't help. This is worth the time and trouble.

Scorpio: Today is a good day to be quiet. Just because someone wants to argue, doesn't mean you have to.

Sagitarius: People will give you bad advice today. It is a good day to spend by yourself.

Capricorn: Today you give up something. But you will get much more in return. The sacrifice is worth it.

Aquarius: Be careful not to be bossy today. You need to be more sympathetic to the people you work with.

Pisces: You can't trust everyone you meet today. Do your own research and think for yourself. Reliable information is important.

Look in today's newspaper and find your horoscope. Compare it to the horoscope listed here. Bring in your horoscope to discuss with the class.

In the following reading, the author, a famous humor writer, talks about her opinion of astrology.

Before you read, think about the following questions.

- Do you read your daily horoscope? If so, do you believe it?
- Do you believe in other kinds of fortune telling, such as psychic advice or palm reading?

Cultural Cues	***Judas Iscariot*** One of the 12 apostles of Jesus, identified as the one who betrayed Jesus for 30 pieces of silver by helping to arrange for his arrest. ***Ann Boleyn*** English queen, the second wife of Henry VIII; within three months, his passion for her had cooled. She was arrested, charged with treason, and beheaded.
About the Author	Erma Bombeck was a columnist and writer who was popular for her humor. She wrote about everyday life, especially that of a wife and mother. Some of her other books include, *At Wit's End, Just Wait Till You Have Children of Your Own!, The Grass Is Always Greener Over the Septic Tank,* and *If Life is a Bowl of Cherries—What Am I Doing in the Pits*? She died in 1996.

by Erma Bombeck Get Off Your Cusp and Live!

Ever since I read that Eva Braun (Hitler's mistress), **Judas Iscariot,** and **Anne Boleyn** shared my zodiac sign, I could never get too **choked up**[1] about Astrology.

5   Mr. Steve meant well, but he didn't know what a loser I was. My sun never rose on my sign. My planets were always **conspiring**[2] behind my back. And my destiny always read like it had been out in the **natal**[3] sun too long.

Maybe I was just bitter, but it always seemed like other people got the good signs. Their horoscopes always read "Popularity and untold wealth will haunt you. There is no getting away from it. You are irresistible to every
10 sign in the zodiac. Give in and enjoy."

Not mine. It was always an **ominous**[4] warning like "Watch your purse." "Your high school acne was only **in remission**[5], and will return the fifteenth of the month." "Don't become discouraged by your friends who will take advantage of you."

15 Somehow, I always felt if Mother had held on a little longer—a good month and a half—things would have been different for me.

Oh, I had faith in the predictions. It was just that my interpretation of my sign was not always the way it turned out. For example:

Prediction: "You get a chance today to provide guidance and
20 **inspiration**[6]."

[1]choked up = emotional
[2]conspiring = planning bad things
[3]natal = related to birth
[4]ominous = threatening, dark
[5]in remission = temporarily cured
[6]inspiration = motivation

Fact: I **chaperoned**[7] thirty fourth-graders on a tour of a meat-packing plant.

Prediction: "One you thought had abandoned you is back in the picture."

25   *Fact:* We found a roach under the sink.

Prediction: "Married or single, this is a 'power' time for you!"

Fact: The heat went off for four hours.

Prediction: "You have a unique way of expressing yourself, and you could gain much satisfaction by writing."

30   *Fact:* I wrote a check to have the **septic tank**[8] cleaned.

Mr. Steve didn't tell me that keeping up with my stars was a full-time job. The daily forecast in the paper was brief and **scanty**[9]. I had to buy a magazine to find out my food forecast, one for my sex forecast, one for my fashion predictions, another for my travel, and still another for my decoration
35   sense, color selection, and perfume.

I wanted to clean out my refrigerator one day but didn't dare because my sign said avoid the color green.

I canceled trips, put off foot surgery, didn't invite Virgos to my party, and on the advice of my horoscope did not handle money for an entire
40   month. (If it hadn't been for my charge card, I'd have died.) There was so much to learn about myself. I was absolutely fascinating. I discovered women born under my sign were dynamic, confident, and into asparagus. I was an orange person, trusting, French **provincial**[10] with **boundless**[11] energy, and **long-waisted**[12].

45   One evening at a jewelry party, one of the brownies I was serving dropped on the carpet. I reached over, picked it up off the floor, popped it in my mouth, and said, "A fuzzy brownie never hurt anyone."

A woman I knew only as Nicky looked deep into my eyes and nodded knowingly. "Only a Pisces **on the cusp**[13] would say that."

50   I asked her how she knew. She said certain **traits**[14] belonged to certain signs. According to my birth date, I was born on a **rising sign**[15] which made my destiny special. I was a wonderful homemaker, excellent cook, and fine seamstress. That wasn't a destiny. It was a sentence!

Source: *Aunt Erma's Cope Book*

---

[7]chaperoned = adult who watches over younger people at social events

[8]septic tank = part of a sewage system for household waste

[9]scanty = meager, not enough

[10]provincial = from a province, the countryside

[11]boundless = endless

[12]long-waisted = the characteristic of a tall, thin person

[13]on the cusp = born on the day that a sun sign moves into a new sign

[14]traits = characteristics, qualities

[15]rising sign = an astrology term

Check Your Comprehension

1. How does Bombeck interpret the predictions in her horoscope?

2. Where does the author read about her horoscope?

3. What does this quotation mean: "Somehow, I always felt if Mother had held on a little longer—a good month and a half—things would have been different for me."

4. How does the author feel about horoscopes in general?

5. What do the last statements, "That wasn't a destiny. It was a sentence!" mean? What is the special meaning of the word "sentence" here?

READING

Find out more about **understanding humor** by looking in the Reference Guide to Reading Strategies on pages xii–xiv.

Understanding Humor

This essay uses humor to make its main points. Can you understand how the following passages are intended to be humorous? Write a brief explanation of the humor after each passage.

1. I wanted to clean out my refrigerator one day but didn't dare because my sign said avoid the color green.

   _____

   _____

2. *Prediction:* "One you thought had abandoned you is back in the picture."
   Fact: We found a roach under the sink.

   _____

   _____

3. Somehow, I always felt if Mother had held on a little longer—a good month and a half—things would have been different for me.

   _____

   _____

4. I was a wonderful homemaker, excellent cook, and fine seamstress. That wasn't a destiny. It was a sentence!

   _____

   _____

Discuss your answers with your classmates.

VOCABULARY
Using Phrases

The following phrases are found in the reading. Show that you understand how to use them by filling the correct prepositions in the blanks. You will use some of the prepositions more than once.

> *about*   *in*   *out*   *off*   *with*
>
> *on*   *of*   *for*   *to*   *up*   *at*

1. I get choked _____ _____ sad movies.

2. Don't tell me the ending, I want to see for myself how it turns

_____ .

3. My sister's old boyfriend is back _____ the picture—they had a date last week.

4. Be careful not to let people take advantage _____ you.

5. The alarm went _____ every time someone walked by the car.

6. My brother said that I should have faith _____ my abilities.

7. My sister runs so fast I can't keep _____ _____ her.

8. What did you find _____ _____ the new secretary?

9. My father told us to clean _____ our closets and get rid

_____ our old toys.

10. I really don't want to study, so I'll put it _____ _____ another hour.

11. _____ the advice _____ my doctor, I'm going to stop smoking.

12. According _____ my teacher, class is canceled tomorrow.

13. If it hadn't been _____ that party Saturday, the whole weekend would have been boring.

THINK ABOUT IT

1. Do you share the author's opinion about horoscopes? Why or why not?

2. Find today's horoscopes in the newspaper and read them. Do they sound accurate? Why or why not?

3. If a fortune teller or your horoscope told you there would be a horrible car accident if you went out, would you stay home? Why or why not?

PART TWO

Unidentified Flying Objects
Life Out There

People around the world are fascinated by the idea of life on other planets.
In the United States, many organizations and groups focus their attention
on this issue. But, so far, no contact has been made . . .
at least we don't *think* so.

Before You Read

Participants in the 50th anniversary Roswell UFO parade.

In the following reading, the author discusses Roswell, New Mexico, where
50 years ago, some people believe that a spaceship crashed.

Before you read, think about the following questions:

- Do you believe in life in outer space?

- Have you ever seen something in the sky that you couldn't explain?

 Watch the
CNN video
on Roswell,
New Mexico.
Discuss these questions:

1. What happened in
   Roswell, new Mexico?

2. How does the United
   States Air Force
   explain the event?

3. Do you believe a
   flying saucer crashed
   in Roswell?

144

READING

Find out more about **increasing speed** by looking in the Reference Guide to Reading Strategies on pages xii–xiv.

Increasing Speed

Record the time it takes you to read this article. Try to read as quickly as you can while still understanding the story.

Starting Time: _____:_____

Cultural Cues

UFO Unidentified Flying Object.

Wal-Mart A large discount store chain.

ROSWELL, NEW MEXICO: Home of the Strange
by Laura Bly

Most people in this little town of 50,000 never thought much about the "Incident." Nearly fifty years ago, there was a **fiery**[1] crash landing. The U.S. Army first said it was a flying
5 saucer. However, the next day they said it was a lost weather balloon.

But now, Stan Crosby and his neighbors are cashing in on the fad for extraterrestrials. The 49th anniversary of the Roswell crash and
10 the alien-invasion film *Independence Day* will bring at least 10,000 people to the city's second "**UFO** Encounter."

There will be an alien costume contest and an "out of this world" fireworks display. Tour-
15 ists will visit the International UFO Museum and Research Center, one of two Roswell museums featuring visitors from outer space. For $15 per person, they will take an 8-mile drive to the place where two alien spacecraft are
20 said to have collided.

This collision began the 50-year controversy.

On July 8, 1947, the Roswell *Daily Record* reported the military's capture of a flying sau-
25 cer. But then officials changed their minds. The next day they said it was a "harmless, high-altitude weather balloon." Most citizens believed them.

However, in the 1980s, books, articles, and
30 TV shows suggested a military cover-up. A New Mexico politician asked for an investigation. The investigators reported that the Roswell crash was a spy device. They said it was designed to learn whether the Soviets were test-
35 ing atomic weapons. There was one problem, however: the officials admitted that records from the Roswell military base—1946 to 1950—couldn't be located. More people began believing in the UFO theory. Because of this, some
40 Roswell residents were afraid of their town being called "**Kook**[2] City."

"But once people saw we weren't sacrific-

---

[1]fiery = on fire, blazing

ing UFO babies on the courthouse lawn, they calmed down," Crosby says.

45 These days, the "Kook City" fears are mostly gone. They've been replaced with the knowledge that tourists mean good business.

The local **Wal-Mart** store ordered "impact site" T-shirts, and the Roswell Inn says about 50 15% of its summer business is UFO fans.

At the International UFO Museum and Research Center, a silver saucer pokes through the roof. About 350 visitors a day come to look at fuzzy photos and UFO-related news articles. 55 Admission is free, but it costs $2.50 to have your picture taken with an alien dummy. A few blocks down Main Street, the UFO **Enigma**[3] Museum attracts more tourists because of a **fiberglass**[4] saucer surrounded by stuffed 60 aliens.

Among the recent visitors were Rufus and Helen Davidson of Florida. Like so many others who come to UFO Town, USA, the Davidsons say they experienced something they can't ex-65 plain.

"We saw one in Ohio back in 1964 or '65," Rufus remembers. "It was bullet-shaped . . . and it was not a weather balloon, I can guarantee that."

70 No matter what the Davidsons saw, Stan Crosby is happy to keep the questions—and the possibilities—alive.

"We've always been a flow-through point to somewhere else," he acknowledges.

75 Until now: "Everybody loves a mystery, and we're playing along. . . . We were given a lemon, and we're making lemonade."

[2]kook = crazy person
[3]enigma = an unexplained event, something puzzling
[4]fiberglass = a type of building material similar to plastic

Source: *USA Today*

Ending Time: ____:____

minus starting time: _____

515 ÷ _____

Total Mins. = words per minute

Compare your reading rate with the one you had on page 98. Is it faster? How much? What is your goal for your speed?

Check Your Comprehension

1. What is the "Incident"?

2. What does "Kook City" mean? Why did this term worry some of the residents?

3. What does "impact site" mean?

4. Why do some people believe that the military is hiding the truth?

5. What does the last sentence, "We were given a lemon, and we're making lemonade," mean?

6. Why are some Roswell residents happy about the stories about aliens?

VOCABULARY
Defining Words from Context

Look back at the reading and find the following words and phrases. Then write a definition of each one. Don't look at your dictionary; try to use the text around the words to help you understand their meaning.

1. flying saucer _____

   _____

2. weather balloon _____

   _____

3. outer space _____

   _____

4. cash in on _____

   _____

5. flow-through point _____

   _____

6. enigma _____

   _____

7. dummy _____

   _____

8. alien _____

   _____

THINK ABOUT IT

1. Why do you think people are so fascinated by the idea of UFOs?

2. Which do you believe—the government story or the local people who believe there was a UFO crash?

3. Mr. Crosby said in the article, "Everybody loves a mystery." What other mysteries interest people? What mysteries interest you?

Before You Read

Does this look like a UFO to you?

The following article talks about SETI, the search for extraterrestrial intelligence.

Before you read, think about the following questions:
- Do you believe there is intelligent life in outer space?
- Do you enjoy science fiction books and movies?

READING

Find out more about **skimming** by looking in the Reference Guide to Reading Strategies on pages xii–xiv.

Skimming

Read this passage in *two* minutes. Then write three main ideas from the reading on the lines below.

1. _____

2. _____

3. _____

Cultural Cues

NASA National Aeronautics and Space Administration, the U.S. space agency.

McDonnell Douglas A large aerospace engineering company.

SETI
(The Search for Extraterrestrial Intelligence)

It seems that people have long dreamed and wondered about the existence of life on other planets. We're especially interested in knowing whether this life can communicate with us. Over the past 50 years, with the help of radio telescopes, we now have the technology to allow **interplanetary**[1]
5   communication. The question is, will we find someone to communicate with?

We are also fascinated with the idea of space travel. Although astronauts have walked on the moon, we now hope to visit other communities on planets and moons even farther away. Dr. William A. Gaubatz from the
10   **McDonnell Douglas** Aerospace division has offered the idea that "Space is a Place." By this he means that space may be the place to travel, play, work, build things, and mine minerals and convert them into energy.

What would life be like if we really had a space transportation system that could carry us to other planets? How long will it be until we have farms
15   on the moon or space tourism? Maybe there will be television shows from Mars. Maybe new "pioneers" will build new communities in space. This outlook believes that space should be explored. It is the dream of a new frontier to learn about and delight in, and a chance perhaps to encounter and investigate other life forms.
20   One group that holds these dreams is the SETI Institute, in Mountain View, California. This institute is the home for scientific and educational projects focusing on the presence of life in the universe. The Institute conducts and encourages research in a large number of fields, including **astronomy**[2] and the planetary sciences, evolution, and the origin of life.
25   The Institute also encourages public information and education programs that teach people about SETI.

The institute's projects have been sponsored by **NASA,** the National Science Foundation, the Department of Energy, the U.S. Geological Survey, private industry, and private donations.
30   So, it seems that many people, from private citizens to large government agencies, are interested in finding life in space. A film, *Contact*, was made in 1997 about SETI. In it, the main character Ellie Arroway, a SETI scientist, defends a request for money to do her research:

[1]interplanetary = between planets
[2]astronomy = the study of stars and planets

Executive: We must confess that your proposal seems less like science
and more like science fiction.

35

Ellie Arroway: Science fiction. You're right, it's crazy. In fact, it's
even worse than that, it's nuts. You wanna hear something really
nutty? I heard of a couple guys who wanna build something
called an airplane, you know you get people to go in, and fly
around like birds, it's ridiculous, right? And what about breaking
the sound barrier, or rockets to the moon? Atomic energy, or
a mission to Mars? Science fiction, right? Look, all I'm asking is
for you to just have the tiniest bit of vision. You know, to just
sit back for one minute and look at the big picture. To take a
chance on something that just might end up being the most
profoundly impactful moment for humanity, for the history . . .
of history.

40

45

Only the future will tell if we will find life in space, and whether we will
go to meet it.

Check Your Comprehension

1. What technology will allow us to talk to other communities in space?

2. What are some of the activities that Dr. Gauvatz suggests for outer space?

3. What activities does the SETI institute sponsor?

4. Who has sponsored some of the SETI Institute's activities? Why is this important?

5. Who is interested in finding life in space?

6. Who is Ellie Arroway?

7. How does she try to convince the executive that SETI is worth supporting?

VOCABULARY
Definitions

Look up these words in the dictionary. Rewrite the definitions in your own words. Write an example sentence that shows you understand the meaning of the word.

1. interplanetary

Definition: _____

_____

Example: _____

_____

2. astronauts

Definition: _____

_____

Example: _____

_____

3. aerospace

Definition: _____

_____

Example: _____

_____

4. astronomy

Definition: _____

_____

Example: _____

_____

5. planetary

Definition: _____

_____

Example: _____

_____

6. evolution

Definition: _____

_____

Example: _____

_____

THINK ABOUT IT

1. What do you know about the existence of life elsewhere in the universe, based on book, television, and movies.

2. Do you believe that extraterrestrials have visited our planet?

3. Imagine the following situation:

   The SETI radio telescopes have picked up unusual radio signals from deep space. The analysis of the signals shows that the signals come from intelligent life on a distant planet.

   You would like to communicate with this life-form.

   What message will you send?

   What kind of communication you will use? (computer, music, language, etc.).

   Explain your choice.

S Y N T H E S I S

Discussion and Debate

1. Some people find astrology to be "harmless fun;" others believe it can be a damaging superstition. What do you think?

2. Billions of dollars are spent to explore space and search for intelligent life in space. Is this money well spent? Or, should this money be used for projects here on earth? What benefit does space exploration bring us?

3. Is there a connection between the belief in aliens and the belief in astrology, in your opinion?

4. Think of another question to ask your classmates about the ideas in this chapter.

Writing Topics

1. In your journal, write about what you think of when you look at the moon or stars.

2. With a group of people, imagine that you are pioneers who have been asked to establish a community on another planet. What will you take with you? Write a plan for your community. Food and water will be provided, but all other materials you must request.

3. If you had to leave earth and live on another planet, where would you live? Why? Write an essay in which you discuss your choice. What do you imagine life will be like?

On Your Own

1. Interview five people. Ask them the following questions, and any other questions you want to add:

   • Do you believe in astrology?

   • Do you read your horoscope?

- Do you believe in life on other planets?
- Have you ever seen a UFO?

Compare your answers to ones that your classmates got. What conclusions can you draw?

2. If possible, find out more about SETI on the Internet and record some notes about what you find to share with your class.

3. Watch one of these movies, which focus on communicating with people in outer space: *Contact; E.T., The Extra-Terrestrial; Close Encounters of the Third Kind.* Report on the movie to your class.

★★★

A L M A N A C For additional cultural information, refer to the Almanac on pages 217–228. The Almanac contains lists of useful facts, maps, and other information to enhance your learning.

★★

CHAPTER 8

Entertainment

The United States is famous for entertainment—in fact, music, movies, and television shows are its biggest export to the rest of the world. Just as entertainment reflects American culture, it also affects the world culture.

PART ONE

Music: Getting Into the Swing of It

America's mix of cultures have had a tremendous effect on its musical history. One of the strongest influences has come from types of music that were first played by African Americans—jazz, blues, and rock and roll. These musical forms have been much admired and imitated around the world.

Before You Read

Benny Goodman

Louis Armstrong

Do you know what kind of music these people play?

In this reading, we will look at the history of jazz in one city: New Orleans, Louisiana. New Orleans is an important center for jazz, even today.

Before you read, think about these questions:

- What types of American music do you enjoy?
- Which American musicians are your favorites?

Cultural Cues

Civil War The American Civil War, which started in 1861 and ended in 1865; the Civil War began when the southern states declared independence from the North. A major issue in the war was slavery.

Louis Armstrong A famous jazz musician; "Satchmo" was born in 1900 and died in 1971. He was famous for his rough-sounding voice and his trumpet playing.

About the Author

Watch the CNN video on world jazz.

Discuss these questions:

1. Why is jazz music less popular in the U.S. than in the rest of the world?

2. What kinds of activities happen at the conference?

3. Who are the musicians in this story?

Langston Hughes was born in 1902 and died in 1967. He was a leader of a social movement called the *Harlem Renaissance*. He wrote poetry, children's books, and music. He was a powerful voice that spoke out for African Americans in the United States.

by Langston Hughes # Old New Orleans

A hundred and fifty years ago in old New Orleans there was a public square called Congo Square. It was a big wide open dusty place where on Sundays, when they did not have to work, the African slaves came with their drums to sing and dance what they called the bamboula. Crowds used to gather
5 around the square to watch the dancing slaves and listen to the music that they made on their drums. This was mostly rhythm music, unless sometimes the dancers began to sing or to chant remembered African songs against the drums, or to make up words of their own. Long after the time of the **Civil War** these Sunday dances continued. Little **Louis Armstrong**'s great-
10 grandmother remembered them well and told him about the dreams.
Most people who write about the history of American jazz believe that

jazz began in New Orleans, where the bands and **orchestras**[1] borrowed some of the rhythms of the drums in Congo Square. The rhythms that the drummers there beat out in the dusty sunlight made the people standing around want to move their heads in time, tap their feet, and dance, too. That is one of the things about jazz: it always makes people want to move. Jazz music is music to move to, to dance to—not just to listen to.

The African drummers in New Orleans did not have any written music. They played from memory or made up rhythms as they went along, since they were playing just for fun. Today the best jazz is often played without music, from a tune remembered, and played as one feels like playing it for fun at that particular moment.

New Orleans had been a French city and a Spanish city before it was an American city, so, in addition to the slave drums, it knew many different kinds of music, both popular and classical. There was a great opera house in New Orleans long before the Civil War. And there were very fine orchestras and bands in the Louisiana city. But many people could not afford to go to the opera house, or listen to the symphony orchestras, or learn to play music by note as trained musicians did. So the poor people, without teachers, made their own music, playing mostly by ear for fun the melodies of old Spanish songs and French dance quadrilles and putting behind them the beat of Congo Square drums—which made this freshly made up early music of New Orleans a very lively music indeed.

Old New Orleans had many marching bands that played a louder, livelier, more steadily rhythmical music than orchestras in opera houses or concert halls, and folks almost danced when they marched along behind such bands. On the sidewalks children did dance. When Louis Armstrong's parents were young, these brass bands often played in the streets or in parks where everybody could hear them for nothing. The sidewheel steamers that paddled up and down the Mississippi River from New Orleans to Memphis and St. Louis carried little bands on them. So the lively drum-time marching music of New Orleans, many years ago, began to spread all over the heart of America. And it turned into dancing music. Its **syncopated**[2] 1–2–3–4 beat, a particular kind of 1–2–3–4 beat played with the accent shifted to the weak beat and stepped up a bit by memories of Congo Square, became a part of jazz.

Source: *The First Book of Jazz*

[1]orchestras = musical groups
[2]syncopated = short, compressed

Check Your Comprehension

1. Who were the first jazz musicians?

2. What is the *bamboula*?

3. Before New Orleans was an American city, what kind of city was it?

4. What countries' music contributed to jazz?

5. Why did jazz become popular?

6. Describe how African drummers in New Orleans played.

7. How did jazz spread throughout the United States?

8. What other kinds of music were found in earlier times in the United States?

 READING

Find out more about **summarizing** by looking in the Reference Guide to Reading Strategies on pages xii–xiv.

Summarizing

This reading focuses on the history of early jazz. Summarize this story in the following box. Don't use more space than that!

Now, compare your summary with one a classmate wrote. Answer these questions:

• What information did you include that your partner did not?

• If you could rewrite your summary, what would you change?

VOCABULARY
Idioms

Many phrases in English are idioms; that is, the meanings of the individual words may not tell you the meaning of the whole idiom. For example, look at this sentence:

My chances of getting a job *went up in smoke.*

Can you guess what "went up in smoke" means? To *go up in smoke* means to disappear, almost instantly. Do you understand why the idiom means this?

Find the following idioms in the reading. (The idioms in the sentences below are in *italics*.) After you discover what they mean, write a new sentence, using the idiom correctly.

1. to *make up* something (you can also say *to make something up*) _____

_____

2. *just for fun* _____

_____

3. hear them *for nothing* _____

_____

4. *play by ear* _____

_____

THINK ABOUT IT

1. Langston Hughes says that jazz made people in New Orleans feel like dancing. What kind of music makes you want to dance? What kind makes you happy? Sad?

2. Write about music. Here are some ideas to get you started:
   - Describe a kind of music you like and a kind that you dislike.
   - Write about your favorite musician.
   - What's your favorite song today? What was your favorite song last year?
   - Can you play the piano? Do you like to sing?

3. Jazz is known as an American form of music. What type of music is your culture known for? Do you know the history of that type of music? Discuss this topic with your classmates.

4. This reading gives many vocabulary items that can be organized into *categories*. Can you fit the words into the right categories? Refer to the reading for help. Then, add two new items in each category. Some examples are given for you.

Type of musical instrument	Type of music	Type of dance	American states	American cities
A drum	Jazz	The bamboula	Louisiana	New Orleans
				Memphis
				St. Louis

Before You Read

A   B   C   D

E   F   G   H

This article discusses the importance of music from the African American community in the United States. Can you match the musicians in the photographs with the types of music they perform? Put the letter of the musician next to the type of music. Some will have more than one letter.

1. _____ rock and roll

2. _____ blues

3. _____ jazz

4. _____ pop

Before you read this article, think about these questions:

• Do you know of any African American musicians?

• How many styles of American music can you name?

• Consider the following quotation from jazz musician Charlie Parker (1920-1955): "Music is your own experience, your own thoughts, your wisdom. If you don't live it, it won't come out of your horn." What do you think Parker means by this?

Cultural Cues

Nat "King" Cole and **Ella Fitzgerald** early jazz singers.

Louis Armstrong early jazz artist.

Miles Davis the inventor of "cool" jazz.

Bob Marley a reggae singer.

James Brown, Little Richard, Chuck Berry early rock and roll artists.

B.B King a blues guitarist and singer.

Sarah Vaughn and **Billie Holiday** early jazz singers.

Aretha Franklin and Diana Ross rock and roll singers who began their careers in the 1960s.

Michael Jackson a pop singer who started his career in the 1960s when he was a child.

SPIRITUALS TO HIP HOP:
THE IMPORTANCE OF BLACK MUSIC IN AMERICA

June is Black Music Month in the United States. Each year at this time, the music industry recognizes and highlights the important contributions made by African-Americans to 5 the development of music in America.

Music has always been a compelling part of the African-American experience. Black music in America dates back to the work songs of the enslaved Africans who were forced to 10 work for white farmers. These slaves sang songs to help the time go faster, to communicate with one another in the fields, and to talk to God about their problems. By the late 1800's, this music had begun to evolve into the forms

15 we know today as the blues and jazz. And 100 years later, black performers like Whitney Houston, Janet Jackson, and Boys II Men are not only at the forefront of the American music scene, but have also become world-famous en-
20 tertainers.

Many Europeans thought of music only as an art form, and therefore a luxury solely intended for the rich. Blacks, on the other hand, whether in Africa or America, used music in
25 much more practical ways. The song "Follow the Drinking Gourd" included directions to slaves about how to escape from their captors. The blues offered a kind of self-help system for dealing with problems. Gospel music was
30 used in religious ceremonies to praise God, and in everyday life to help people keep their hopes up.

The history of American Black music is a long one. And throughout that history, African-
35 Americans have been at the **cutting edge**[1] of musical innovation. In fact, this one group of people is largely responsible for the growth of,

and present size of, the popular music industry in the United States today. From gospel, blues,
40 and jazz, to rock and roll, rap, and hip hop, African-Americans have helped to define the American musical experience.

When Americans celebrate Black music month, they celebrate the contributions of
45 early jazz singers like Ella Fitzgerald, Sarah Vaughn, Billie Holiday and **Nat King Cole.** Also remembered are **Louis Armstrong** and **Miles Davis,** two horn players who changed jazz history. **James Brown, Little Richard,**
50 and **Chuck Berry** were early rock and roll musicians who shocked some and excited millions with their wild new musical style. Other major contributors include **Bob Marley,** a reggae artist whose son Ziggy continues his tradi-
55 tion, and **B.B. King,** a blues guitarist. And we can't forget **Aretha Franklin, Diana Ross,** and **Michael Jackson,** world-famous pop stars who deserve the fame they have gained for their music.
60 Many would argue there would be no American music without African-American music. June is the month to remember those who have changed musical history.

[1]cutting edge = forefront, beginning

Check Your Comprehension

1. What is celebrated in June?
2. Which types of music are considered "black" music?
3. What was the difference in attitudes towards music in some European and African American communities?
4. How did black music start in the United States?
5. What does "cutting edge" mean? How does it relate to this story?

 READING

Find out more about **understanding the main point** by looking in the Reference Guide to Reading Strategies on pages xii–xiv.

Understanding the Main Point

Although this reading mentions many different ideas about music, it has one main idea. What is that idea? Try to express it in one sentence.

_____

_____

Compare your sentence with a classmate's. Did you come up with the same idea? Discuss your ideas with your classmates.

VOCABULARY
Musical Vocabulary

Do you know what these kinds of music are? Begin by stating what you already know. Then, look up their dictionary definitions. Write a short description of each below.

blues _____

_____

_____

jazz _____

_____

_____

gospel _____

_____

_____

rock & roll _____

_____

_____

hip hop _____

_____

_____

You might learn more by trying to find examples of this music. Check a local radio guide, or ask your friends and family if they have any recordings of these kinds of music. Try to listen to as many examples as you can.

THINK ABOUT IT

1. Although many of the types of music listed in this reading are identified as "American" music, they are written and performed in other countries, too. Which kinds of music mentioned in this article have been accepted in your home culture?

2. Do you have a favorite kind of American music? Which musicians do you admire most?

3. What kind of traditional music is your home country known for? If you have any recordings, bring them to class to play and discuss with your classmates

4. Watch a music video on TV (look at MTV, VH1 or BET for videos if you can). What was it like? Did you enjoy it?

PART TWO

SPORTS: It's How You Play the Game

Sports are an important form of entertainment in the United States.
Millions of people play baseball, basketball, football, and even soccer.
Millions more watch these games on television.

Before You Read

Have you seen a basketball game? What about a women's basketball game? In the following reading, you will read an interview conducted on the Internet with one of the most famous women basketball players, Rebecca Lobo.

Before you read, think about the following questions:

- Do you enjoy sports?
- Have you ever played basketball?
- Have you ever watched women's sporting events?

Rebecca Lobo

Cultural Cues

NCAA National Collegiate Athletic Assocation.

Larry Bird A former professional basketball player for the Boston Celtics, now the coach of the National Basketball Association (NBA) team, the Indiana Pacers.

Dr. J A former professional basketball player, Julius Erving, of the Philadelphia 76ers.

Carlton Fisk A baseball player with the Boston Red Sox, 1969–1980 and the Chicago White Sox, 1981–1991.

MVP Most Valuable Player.

165

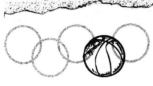 An Interview With **Rebecca Lobo**

The following is part of an interview that took place on the Internet. It's called a "Golden Moment Chat," and this one is with U.S. Olympic Basketball team member, Rebecca Lobo. The television network NBC conducted this interview during the Olympic Games.

5   Rebecca Lobo helped the University of Connecticut win the 1995 **NCAA** title and was named the tournament's Most Outstanding Player. She has become one of the country's most prominent representatives of women's basketball. She is now a member of the WNBA, Women's National Basketball Association, playing for the New York Liberty.

10 *NBC Host:* Rebecca, thank you so much for coming on-line with us today! We really appreciate your taking the time out during these exciting Games and coming on-line to chat with your **cyberfans**[1]. Let's get started with our first question.

NBC Host: What does it feel like to play in the Olympics?

15 *Rebecca:* It's an incredible **rush**[2] and especially to play in front of large crowds and know that you're representing your country.

NBC Host: Your team is **faring**[3] very well in the games. Do you feel that you are being overshadowed by the men's team or do you think the women's team is receiving its fair share of attention?

20 *Rebecca:* Our past two games we have set two new attendance records for women's sports so we feel our game is coming into our own. We feel there is room for both the women and men to play and receive their share of attention.

NBC Host: As a child, what did you want to be when you grew up?

25 *Rebecca:* I always wanted to play basketball as far as I can remember. I dreamed of playing for the Boston Celtics. When I got older, I thought about becoming a lawyer or a teacher or some other profession.

NBC Host: How many hours do you practice without your team?

Rebecca: This year most of the things we do are with the team. We practice
30   almost five hours a day. In the off season, I practice three to four hours, which includes basketball, conditioning, and weight lifting.

NBC Host: Who do you feel is your team's **MVP**?

---

[1]cyberfans = fans on the Internet
[2]rush = slang for "excitement"
[3]faring = doing

Rebecca: We have so many different contributors, everyone has shined this year. I think Teresa and Katrina are our leaders and the heart and soul
35 of this team.

NBC Host: Australia looked like they might just give the Team a run for their money, but you guys were able to control and walk away. What do you view as the greatest challenge still before you on the road to the gold medal?

40 *Rebecca:* Brazil, who is also undefeated, will be a big challenge. Without overlooking other games, we might face Australia again and they may give us another test!

NBC Host: When did you start basketball? Did you play all through grade school?

45 *Rebecca:* The first team I was on was in the third grade and I played every year, and every summer, after that!

NBC Host: Congratulations to you and all the members of the women's basketball team. With the increased awareness of women's basketball in this country, what are your feelings about the success of women's
50 professional basketball in this country?

Rebecca: I'm very excited about the increased interest and I think it will carry over into the professional game and carry over to that level.

NBC Host: Rebecca—What are you going to do after the Games? Are you going to continue with basketball or take some time off to pursue some-
55 thing else?

Rebecca: I'm going to take a little time off. But a little time only means about a month. I plan on continuing my career as long as my body allows me to!

NBC Host: Rebecca, do you find it distracting with all the media?

60 *Rebecca:* Not at all, they are only allowed to be around us at certain times. I remember when there were only two people following the women's game. I would much rather have it like this.

NBC Host: Which is your favorite moment in the Olympic Games so far?

Rebecca: Opening ceremonies and each of our games has been very special
65 also!

NBC Host: With so much of your time being devoted to basketball how do you manage to lead a normal life?

Rebecca: It's not completely normal, but I make sure I find the time for my family and friends and always make sure I have time for myself!

70 *NBC Host:* Rebecca . . . where did you get your good looks?

Rebecca: I appreciate the compliment! I get half from my mother and half from my father!

NBC Host: What separates the Olympic class athlete from the rest? Is it more mental discipline, focus, and toughness, or is it more natural talent?

75 *Rebecca:* It's a combination of all three, plus an incredible commitment.

NBC Host: Who is your all time favorite sports figure?

Rebecca: In basketball, I grew up watching **Larry Bird** and **Dr. J** and I loved watching **Carlton Fisk.** I appreciated all sports figures and never really had an all-time favorite.

80 *NBC Host:* Rebecca, thank you so much for coming on-line today and talking to all your cyberfans out here! Good luck in your quest for the Gold!

Rebecca: I appreciate everyone typing in and I hope you keep watching our Games!

Source: *NBC "Golden Moments" interviews*

Check Your Comprehension

1. What does Ms. Lobo like about playing in the Olympics?

2. How was the attendance at the Olympics for women's basketball?

3. How much training does Rebecca do every day?

4. According to Ms. Lobo, what qualities are necessary for an Olympic athlete?

5. What was her favorite part of the Olympic Games?

6. What teams does she think will be difficult for the United States to beat?

7. How does she feel about the media?

 **READING**

Find out more about **summarizing** by looking in the Reference Guide to Reading Strategies on pages xii–xiv.

Summarizing

This reading is an interview, so the organization is different from a typical essay. Put the information you learned from reading the interview into summary format. You should have three summaries that focus on the main areas of the interview: Rebecca Lobo's childhood, The Olympic Games, and Life as a Basketball Player.

1. Rebecca Lobo's Childhood _____

_____

2. The Olympic Games _____

_____

3. Life as a Basketball Player _____

_____

VOCABULARY
Slang and Colloquial Language

Review the reading, looking for the following phrases. Discuss their meaning with a classmate. Choose and fill in the phrase that would best complete the sentences. Use each phrase only once.

be an incredible rush   *give us a run for our money*
come into our own   *practice every day in the off season*
fare very well   *receive their fair share of attention*

1. Q: Who will be difficult to beat?

A: Australia will _____

_____ .

2. Q: Do men dominate basketball?

A: Both men and women _____

_____ .

3. Q: How often do you work out?

A: I _____

_____ .

4. Q: Are you excited to play in the Olympics?

A: It will _____

_____ .

5. Q: How will the team do next year?

A: I think we will _____

_____ .

6. Q: You lost the first games, but won the last three. What will happen next?

A: I think we are finally going to _____

_____ .

THINK ABOUT IT

1. Do you think women's basketball will eventually be as successful as men's? Why or why not?

2. Have you ever watched the Olympic Games? What events do you enjoy?

3. What sport do you enjoy most? Do you play or just watch?

Before You Read

The Dallas Cowboys

Gallup Poll

The Gallup Polling agency, a group that asks Americans their opinions on a variety of issues, asked the following question about the Super Bowl: "Which do you personally find more entertaining—the Super Bowl game itself or the advertising commercials that run during the Super Bowl?"

They asked both football fans and those who don't watch football. Here's what they said.

	Total	Football fans
The game itself	46%	68%
The commercials	37%	30%
Don't watch game	15%	1%
No opinion	2%	1%

Are you surprised by these numbers?

Cultural Cues   *Super Bowl* The national championship football game, played in late January.

The Dallas Cowboys
AMERICA'S TEAM

In 1960, the Dallas Cowboys became the National Football League's first successful new team. Clint Murchison Jr. was the new team's owner. Tom Landry was named the head coach.

The team was very successful in the professional football world. How-
5 ever, the "glory years" didn't come easily. In the early 1960s, the Cowboys didn't do well. But in 1966, the Cowboys began a **streak**[1] of twenty winning seasons. That streak included 18 years in the playoffs, five trips to the **Super Bowl,** and victories in Super Bowls VI[2] and XII.

During the 1970s, the Cowboys were led by future Pro Football Hall of
10 Fame members: **quarterback**[3] Roger Staubach, and running back Tony Dorsett. The Cowboys of the 1970s and early 1980s were known as "America's Team." Their team was ahead of almost every other club because of promotions such as their team newspaper, *The Dallas Cowboys Newsweekly*, sales of Cowboys souvenirs and clothes, and the famous Dallas Cowboys
15 cheerleaders.

The Cowboys had their first losing season in two decades in 1986, and did even worse in 1988. The team was sold to Jerry Jones in 1989. Jones chose former University of Miami coach Jimmy Johnson to replace Tom Landry. Landry finished his career with 270 victories. This was the third
20 highest number of wins by any coach in football history.

Johnson's first team won only once in 16 games. However, he made some changes that soon led the Cowboys to championship status in Super Bowl XXVII. They followed with a second world title in Super Bowl XXVIII[4]. In March 1994, college coach Barry Switzer replaced Johnson as the Cowboys'
25 third head coach. The winning continued under Switzer. "The Team of the Nineties" won its third Super Bowl in four years with a 27–17 victory over the Pittsburgh Steelers in Super Bowl XXX.

Its winning streak ended there, however. They didn't reach Super Bowl XXXI or XXXII[5]. Maybe next year.

[1]streak = series

[2]The Super Bowl is marked by Roman Numerals: VI = 6 and XII = 12

[3]quarterback = a position on the football team; one of the most important—the quarterback makes decisions about the plays

[4]XXVIII = 28

[5]XXXI or XXXII = 31 or 32

**Check Your
Comprehension**

1. Who was the most successful coach of the Cowboys?

2. What does the phrase "glory years" mean?

3. Who was the least successful coach of the Cowboys?

4. Apart from winning games, what made the team so successful?

5. What were the Cowboys of the '70s and '80s known as? Why?

**READING**

Find out more about **understanding processes** by looking in the Reference Guide to Reading Strategies on pages xii–xiv.

Understanding Processes

This reading presents a sequence of events, or an historical process. Summarize the reading by putting these events into a time line. Put the date on the line at the left, then a short description of the event at the right. The first one is done for you.

Date	Event
1960	The Cowboys became the NFL's first successful new team.

VOCABULARY
Word Search

The words in this word search are associated with football. You probably won't know what all of them mean, but see if you can find out from a dictionary or from asking a football fan!

```
            K C A B L L U F
          F Z N A B N C D E F E N S E
        B I I C X Q H O D S Z B T A C K L E
      T G U A R D P U G R C A T J I O Y Z X K K A
    R S S J J S Q O A Z I F R I E M W U D Y T R O L
  J Q X K Q O T P N R E D A E L R E E H C V U X E X P
  I E N I L D R A Y Y T F I F F B X O R U S H I N G T E C
R H R P M R I N N S T E F R G E G X U T E A M D W K W N Y B
G K I C K O F F D M E R E G C R H L T N N I W A O N Z A E A
E O D N T C C X T D F B D F R E V I E C E R E D I W I L J C
L G A F T O B T E L A A M F I E L D G O A L Z P I H N T U M
  S A L U E N M N I S C L I P P I N G O I J Q S G X V Y W
    B F P H R E K C I K E C A L P P R L K C H B H W Z A
      S V O K C A B F L A H X Q G L I N E B A C K E R
        V E S S E D I S F F O Y E S F D O Y E I S L
          V T D P W T U U E N O Z D N E R J F
            S X T S S A P L A R E T A L
              D B S C O R E T
```

WORD LIST

blitz	fullback	linebacker	score
center	goal posts	offsides	tackle
cheerleader	gridiron	penalty	team
clipping	guard	placekicker	time out
defense	halfback	quarterback	~~touchdown~~
end zone	intercept	referee	wide receiver
field goal	kickoff	rushing	win
fifty-yard line	lateral pass	safety	wishbone
first and ten			

THINK ABOUT IT

1. Have you seen an American football game? If so, What was it like?

2. Do you watch soccer? Do you like it better than American football?

3. A news reporter recently claimed that football is now America's national sport, overtaking baseball. Which sport characterizes America better, in your opinion?

4. "Super Bowl Sunday," the day on which the national championship game is played, has become almost like a holiday. People often have parties to watch the game, even if they don't like football or their team isn't playing. Talk to someone who has been to a Super Bowl party. Ask them about it.

SYNTHESIS

Discussion and Debate

1. Soccer is a very popular sport, even in the United States. However, it does not receive as much attention in the United States as it does in other countries. Why do you think this is so?

2. Professional sports stars and rock musicians can be paid millions of dollars a year just to play. They also receive millions more to endorse certain products. Do you think stars are paid too much? Why or why not?

3. Is it harder to be a good musician or a good athlete? Why?

4. Think of another question to ask your classmates about the ideas in this chapter.

Writing Topics

1. Write one or two paragraphs describing a favorite entertainment activity in your home country that isn't practiced in the United States.

2. In your journal, write about your favorite music or favorite sport.

3. Is there a musician or a sports figure that you admire? Write an essay in which you talk about why you admire this person; discuss his or her admirable qualities, as well as details about his or her life. You may need to research some facts on the Internet or in a magazine.

On Your Own

1. Find a story in the sports pages that interests you and read it. Summarize the story for your classmates.

2. Watch a movie that focuses on sports. Here are some to consider:

    Bull Durham, Baseball

    Rocky, Boxing

    North Dallas Forty, Football

    A League of Their Own, Baseball

    The Natural, Baseball

    Personal Best, Track and Field

    Tin Cup, Golf

    Chariots of Fire, Track and Field

    Hoop Dreams, Basketball

    White Men Can't Jump, Basketball

    Field of Dreams, Baseball

    Phar Lap, Horse Racing

    When We Were Kings, Boxing

    Bang the Drum Slowly, Baseball

    Barton Fink, Wrestling

    Report to your class on the film you watched.

3. Choose a sport you don't know much about. Do some research about the rules of the game. If you can, attend a game or watch one on television. What was the game like? Could you understand the rules? Did you enjoy it? Report to your class what you learned.

4. Find CDs or tapes in your library or in a record store of some of the following, and listen to them. Relate them to what you have learned about black music in this chapter:

    "Janet," Janet Jackson

    "Kind of Blue," Miles Davis

    "Best Of Ella Fitzgerald & Louis Armstrong"

    "Two Great Guitars," Bo Diddley & Chuck Berry

    "Blues Is King," B.B. King

    Talk about your opinions of the music with your class.

A L M A N A C   For additional cultural information, refer to the Almanac on pages 217–228. The Almanac contains lists of useful facts, maps, and other information to enhance your learning.

★★

CHAPTER 9

Technology

Technology is changing the world. This is nothing new. However, it is interesting to look at the ways that various cultures accept technology—how they use it, live with it, enjoy it, and create it. This chapter focuses on how technology has affected the United States and vice versa.

PART ONE

THE INFORMATION AGE: Too Much Information?

We live in an "age" of information. The Internet, faxes, e-mail, cellular telephones, and other devices are adding to the amount of information we get every day. The United States is affected greatly by this wealth of information. It is changing the ways in which we communicate, work, and live.

Before You Read   **Percentage of U.S. Homes with Different Electronic Devices**

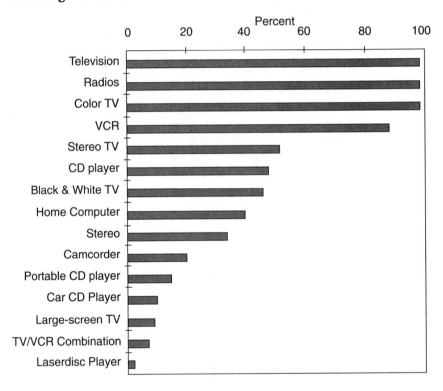

In this article, the writer talks about his involvement with the information revolution.

Before you read, think about the following questions:

• How has technology changed your life?

• Which of the items listed in the graph above are most necessary? Why?

• Have you heard of, or read anything by George Orwell?

Cultural Cues

George Orwell The pseudonym of Eric Arthur Blair, a novelist and essayist, born in Bengal, India, in 1903; his novels *Animal Farm* (1945) and *1984* (1949) are considered classics.

Internal Revenue Service The government agency responsible for collecting taxes.

About the Author

Michael Kinsley is the editor of *Slate*, a magazine that is published on the Internet by Microsoft Corporation.

BY MICHAEL KINSLEY  # ORWELL GOT IT WRONG

George Orwell's famous novel 1984 (written in 1948) opens with its hero, Winston Smith, returning to his **squalid**[1] apartment. Attached to a wall is a "telescreen," described as "an **oblong**[2] metal **plaque**[3] like a dulled mirror." It is in essence a two-way television, which watches Smith's every movement
5 while barking government **propaganda**[4] at him. "Big Brother Is Watching You" is the state's slogan.

This was Orwell's vision of the future: technology would become the tool of totalitarian dictatorship. TV and computers would make Big Brother possible.
10 Fortunately, Orwell got it exactly wrong. The high-tech devices that have invaded our lives—home computers, fax machines, VCRs and now the Internet—have expanded human freedom.

On the Redmond, Washington, campus of Microsoft Corporation, where I work these days, there is not much doubt that technology is a wonderful
15 thing. It has made many of the software programmers, wandering the halls in jeans and T-shirts, rich men and women while still in their 20s or 30s.

But more than that: people in Cyberworld—shorthand for the culture of computers and telecommunications—passionately believe that today's technology revolution is also a revolutionary advance for human liberty.
20 They're right. But most of them also don't remember a time when computers, especially, were thought to be a menace to freedom.

---

[1]squalid = dirty

[2]oblong = long and narrow, like a rectangle

[3]plaque = piece of wood or metal, usually with writing on it

[4]propaganda = political information that is one-sided

Orwell was far from the only doubter of the post-World War I period. During the 1950s and 1960s many other seers worried that ever-bigger computers would lead to centralization of information and power. The **menace**[5]

25 of giant computers was a major theme of popular culture.

Then around 1980, computers suddenly got small. The desktop personal computer (PC) came to market and gave enormous power to the individual. Tiny businesses could do what only large ones could before. Even within big businesses, employees had much more **autonomy**[6]. A symbolic develop-

30 ment was the arrival of inexpensive tax-preparation software. Today you can use your home PC to do your income tax quickly and accurately, while the **Internal Revenue Service** still can't get its own giant computers to work right.

On balance, most people would **concede**[7] that the advantages of today's

35 technologies, including the Internet, outweigh its disadvantages. Certainly our freedom has been **enhanced**[8] on the everyday personal level. (Remember the time before VCRs when you had to watch a TV show or a movie when *they* wanted you to?)

On the more **profound**[9] political level, is there anyone who thinks the

40 world would be a freer place if computers, fax machines and the Internet didn't exist?

Source: *Reader's Digest*

This is one that Orwell really did get wrong.

Check Your Comprehension

1. Who is "Big Brother"?

2. Why does Kinsley think that technology is a "wonderful thing"?

3. What happened to computers in 1980?

4. What was the result of computers becoming smaller?

5. What is "CyberWorld"?

6. Why does the author think that Orwell "got it wrong"?

[5]menace = threat

[6]autonomy = self-sufficiency; self-rule

[7]concede = admit

[8]enhanced = improved

[9]profound = deep

READING

Find out more about **understanding arguments** by looking in the Reference Guide to Reading Strategies on pages xii–xiv.

Understanding Arguments

In this reading, the author makes an argument: "Orwell was wrong."

Review the reading, and list the reasons that the author makes this claim.

Orwell got it wrong. . . .

Reason 1. _____

_____

Reason 2. _____

_____

Reason 3. _____

_____

VOCABULARY
Using New Words

Several words in this reading may not be familiar to you. Complete the following sentences to show that you understand their meaning.

1. A **squalid** room has _____ .

2. I received some **propaganda** that said _____ .

3. I had to **concede** that _____ .

4. A person with **autonomy** doesn't have to _____ .

5. _____ isn't a very **profound** thought.

6. Under a **totalitarian** government, _____ .

THINK ABOUT IT

1. Do you agree with the author? Does technology only expand our freedom? Can you think of examples where it limits our freedom?

2. What technological device has improved your life? What would your life be like without it?

3. What technological device has made your life more difficult? How would your life improve without it?

Before You Read

Spam® is a canned meat product. Spamming is the practice of advertising through unsolicited e-mails.

Computer Words

e-mail: Electronic mail; messages sent using computers.

flame: To insult someone in an e-mail message.

junk mail: Advertising sent through the mail.

net: Short form of the word Internet; the global system of computers, connected by cables and satellites.

spam: Advertising sent through e-mail.

In the following reading, Sanford Wallace and Scott Hazen Mueller discuss "spam," or "junk e-mail." Some people think this type of advertising is the perfect combination of new technology and advertising. Others find it an invasion of privacy.

Before you read, think about the following questions:

- Do you use e-mail? If so, have you received "spam"?
- What is your opinion of "junk mail"—advertising sent without requesting it—either on the Internet or in your mailbox?

READING

Find out more about **skimming** by looking in the Reference Guide to Reading Strategies on pages xii–xiv.

Skimming

Skim the article—that is, read it quickly to get the main idea. Take only two minutes. Answer the following questions after you have read it.

What is Sanford Wallace's view of spamming? _____

_____

What is Scott Mueller's view of spamming? _____

_____

Cultural Cues

Super Bowl The national championship game for U.S. football teams; it is played in January, and is the most popular television show of the year.

pyramid schemes Illegal business structures that rely on people investing their money and bringing in more partners, who then invest their money; no products are created.

Bud's frogs Television advertising for Budweiser beer that features frogs; it was a very successful advertising campaign.

About the Authors

Sanford Wallace is the head of Cyber Promotions, a company that uses the Internet to help companies advertise their products. Scott Hazen Mueller is the Vice President of Engineering for Whole Earth Networks, an Internet Service Provider.

Return to Sender ?
by Sanford Wallace and Scott Hazen Mueller

Is junk e-mail a form of trespassing?

Wallace: Are television ads **trespassing**[1]? Is postal junk mail trespassing? No, because advertising is an accepted part of those media. Since e-mail is a relatively new way to communicate, we're still debating its appropriate uses. Cyber Promotions takes the position that e-mail is no more **exempt**[2] from ads than the **Super Bowl** is from **Bud's frogs.** Commercials are just part of life. In the same way that sponsors help

5

[1]trespassing = illegally entering onto someone's property

[2]exempt = excluded, left out

finance television shows, e-mail advertisement profits will help finance the continued growth and expansion of the Net.

10 *Mueller:* Junk e-mail is more theft than trespassing. You get stuck on a mailing list without having a chance to get off it, and then are **bombarded**[3] with trash that you have to pay for. Think about it–tons of people pay access charges to get this stuff they don't want. They have to **shell out**[4] once to **download**[5] it, and then pay a second time to get
15 on some spammer's "remove" list. No one should ever be sent advertising without their prior permission, and by that I do not mean sending a message to them asking their permission.

Is spamming ever worth it?

Wallace: Absolutely! Many people love to get online breaking news about
20 products, services and opportunities. Also, many **savvy**[6] business people monitor their competitors' e-mail ads to keep tabs on what they're up to. And promotions let you find the best deals, highest-quality products and best services on the Net. The beauty of e-mail advertising is that it is not **intrusive**[7]. Unlike unsolicited phone calls, e-mail doesn't interrupt
25 dinner. E-mail patiently waits until the recipient decides to read it.

Mueller: The only people who benefit from spam are the spammers. I see countless stories about this company or that person who hired a spammer to send their ad. Not only did they not get any sales, they also got flamed in e-mail, they got rude phone calls, and if they gave a fax number, they
30 got even ruder faxes. This is a benefit? The spammers take money from anyone they can find, legitimate or not, and blast mailboxes around the world with **bogus**[8] hair-loss cures, **pyramid schemes** and fake credit repair.

Source: *Time Digital*

Check Your Comprehension

1. What is spam?

2. Why does Mueller think that spam is trespassing?

3. Why does Wallace think it isn't?

4. According to Mueller, who benefits from spam?

5. According to Mueller, why don't merchants benefit from spam?

6. What's a "pyramid scheme"?

[3]bombarded = bombed, overwhelmed
[4]shell out = pay
[5]download = receive from the Internet
[6]savvy = smart
[7]intrusive = invasive, interruptive
[8]bogus = false

VOCABULARY
Slang and Colloquial Language

Match each slang or colloquial word or phrase with its meaning in standard English. Write the letter of the definition in the blank.

_____ **1.** junk mail   **a.** false

_____ **2.** spam   **b.** e-mail advertising

_____ **3.** shell out   **c.** track

_____ **4.** savvy   **d.** insult by e-mail

_____ **5.** keep tabs on   **e.** unwanted advertising

_____ **6.** flame   **f.** pay

_____ **7.** bogus   **g.** knowledgeable

THINK ABOUT IT

1. Do you agree with Wallace or Mueller? Why?

2. Do you agree that e-mail advertising is "not intrusive"? Why or why not?

3. Do you get junk mail? Do you read it? Why or why not?

PART TWO

Virtual Reality: Is It Live or Is It Memorex?

Virtual reality refers to realities created by technology and computers.
Virtual reality might take the form of a game or a simulation on a computer.
It might be a toy or an amusement park ride.

Before You Read

This is an image from a virtual reality program. In this program, you can "walk" through this office park, and look at the buildings, trees, and fountain.

 Watch the CNN video on New York City's Skyride.

Discuss these questions:

1. What is Skyride?

2. What were the passenger's reactions?

3. Would you like to go on Skyride? Why or why not?

In this article, you will read about the use of virtual reality in surgery.

Before you read, think about the following questions:

• Do you know what uses virtual reality has?

• How has technology changed the practice of medicine?

READING

Find out more about **increasing speed** by looking in the Reference Guide to Reading Strategies on pages xii–xiv.

Increasing Speed

Record the time it takes you to read this article. Try to read as quickly as you can while still understanding the story.

Starting Time: ____:____

Cultural Cues

HMO Health maintenance organization, the most common form of private health insurance in the United States.

FDA The Food and Drug Administration, the organization responsible for approving new drugs and medical procedures, as well as regulating the food industry.

VIRTUAL SURGERY

Dr. Kelly, a **neurosurgeon**[1] at New York University Medical Center, prepares for brain surgery by looking through a small hole. "Pretend we're looking into a **spherical**[2] room—like the skull is a spherical room," he said. "And we want to figure out the best way to get to the couch without entering the
5 room—only we want to figure out the best way to get to that deep-seated tumor."

Dr. Kelly moves through the patient's brain, past everything that is blocking the path to the tumor. He is using a computer to do this. In fact, he is one of many doctors in the U.S. developing virtual reality experiments
10 to help plan for surgery. These procedures are approved by the **FDA.**

Like virtual reality programs that allow someone to fly a plane without getting into an airplane, or walk through a new house without leaving the office, the surgery program lets surgeons look through the body and plan the safest method for removing a tumor or repairing an injury. Dr. Kelly
15 treats over 300 patients a year using this new technology.

However, this technology is probably more important than a game or a **flight simulator**[3]. During an operation, a surgeon can sometimes have problems trying to avoid blood vessels. As a result, the patient can suffer

[1]neurosurgeon = doctor who operates on the brain and nervous system
[2]spherical = round
[3]flight simulator = a computer that allows the user to practice flying without an airplane

neurological or **tissue**[4] damage from the operation. But, with computers,
20 using interactive virtual-reality software, the surgeon can plan a surgical
path and think about the operation before any **incision**[5] is made.

Here's how the procedure works.

The doctor performs a CAT (computerized axial tomography) scan,
which produces 500 images of the patient's medical problem. Then, the
25 scans are put into a computer, which processes them into a three-dimen-
sional picture of the patient. Then, the software allows the doctor to "explore" the inside of the patient's problem.

In a study done over 10 years at the Mayo Clinic and New York University
Medical Center, 90 percent of patients who had computer-assisted surgery
30 had their brain tumors completely removed. Those who had traditional
surgery had only a 60 percent removal rate. This fact is very encouraging
for doctors who practice this new surgical method.

However, some doctors prefer the "old" ways. They see the new computer
systems as being nice "toys" but think that their results are overstated. Dr.
35 Fraser, of New York Hospital, stated, "computers are a fun system, but they
make no big difference in patient outcome."

Although some doctors still like the traditional methods, **HMO**s will
soon begin to encourage doctors to use the computerized methods. This is
because they cost less than traditional surgery and patients spend less time
40 in the hospital.

Patients themselves are also demanding this new technology. They have
read about it on the Internet, and want the procedure that is going to work
best and have the least recovery time. In fact, well-informed, technologically
sophisticated[6] patients will probably make the biggest impact on pushing
45 for the advancement of computer-assisted medical treatment.

Source: *New York Cybertimes*

Ending Time: ____:____

minus starting time: _____

492 ÷ _____

Total Mins. = words per minute

Compare your reading rate with the one you had on page 98. Is it faster?
How much? Remember, the typical native speaker of English reads at an
average rate of 250 words per minute. For nonfiction reading, such as this
one, the rate slows down to about 200. You should aim for 150 words per
minute. If your number is a lot slower, practice trying to read faster. (If it's
much faster, you may not be reading carefully enough.) What is your goal
for your speed?

[4]tissue = skin and organs
[5]incision = cut
[6]sophisticated = knowledgeable

Check Your Comprehension

1. Who is Dr. Kelly?
2. What is virtual reality?
3. What is the FDA?
4. How does Dr. Kelly create an image of a patient?
5. Why do HMOs like this new procedure?
6. How much more effective is the new procedure at complete tumor removal?
7. Why do some doctors prefer the "old" ways of surgery?
8. Why do patients want this new technology?

VOCABULARY
Medical Terminology

Below are some medical terms which appear in the article. Be sure you understand what they mean. Look each of them up in a dictionary, and write a definition in your own words.

1. neurosurgeon _____
2. tumor _____
3. injury _____
4. blood vessel _____
5. tissue _____
6. incision _____
7. CAT scan _____
8. tomography _____

THINK ABOUT IT

1. Why do you think Dr. Fraser doesn't like this new surgical method? Are you persuaded by his argument? Why or why not?
2. What is the HMO's biggest concern? Why do you think that is their primary worry?
3. If you needed an operation, would you ask for this type of procedure? Why or why not?

Before You Read

It's a whole new realm...

If you were looking for Denton Online, you can still find it here!

News
Thankfully, the Web site development and Internet Marketing arm of Rick's American Cyber Grill has been very successful. So much so that we have decided to spin this group off as a separate business: New Realm Media Group. We have moved to office space downtown on the square. Look for a new Web site soon that will be unlike anything you've seen on the Internet.

Other Public Internet Access in Denton
There are several places in Denton that offer public Internet access for free. Check out the Emily Fowler Public Library or the Martin Luther King Recreation Center. Soon, the Senior Center will have public access also.

Rick's Grill Home Page: http://www.cybergrill.com

This essay is about cybercafés, a new kind of place where people meet, drink coffee, and surf the Internet.

Before you read, think about the following questions:

- Are there any cybercafés in your town?
- Have you ever visited a cybercafé?

Cultural Cues

Chuck E. Cheese's A popular pizza chain, which focuses on serving children; children go there to play games as well as eat pizza.

Denton A town in Texas near Dallas.

nachos a snack made of tortilla chips, cheese, and other ingredients.

hotlist A list of favorite World Wide Web sites; the hotlist is also a web site that contains links to those web pages.

Netscape A brand of computer software that allows a user to look at web pages.

NASCAR The National Association of Stock Car Auto Racing.

QVC A cable television station on which products are demonstrated, and viewers can buy them by calling a toll-free telephone number.

Chamber of Commerce An association of businesses in a city or town; most cities have a Chamber of Commerce.

Would You Like Nachos or the Internet?
by Todd Copilevitz

Rick and Teresa Hunt have a curious view of how best to negotiate the Net. "There's nothing like a plate of **nachos** to make learning **Netscape** nice and easy," Ms. Hunt explains. If nachos aren't your speed, they can also suggest potato skins, a burger or any of the other several dozen items on the menu
5 at Rick's American Cyber Grill in **Denton** (http://www.cybergrill.com).

Rick's has become a local gathering place, where the regulars surf the Net, research their competition, market their businesses and help others do the same. On any given day, you'll see a mixture of college students, senior citizens and often families whose children find the computers as
10 attractive as the games at **Chuck E. Cheese's**. Only here, the parents find themselves just as **intrigued**[1]. On the East and West coasts, cyber coffeehouses and cafés may be all the rage. Typically they are places where the **digitally**[2] cool stop by for an **espresso**[3], check their e-mail and show off their **hotlist**. But, for reasons no one knows for sure, here in Texas
15 they've never caught on.

But up in Denton, far removed from the traditional urban markets for cyber joints, the Hunts assembled a **network**[4] of five computers in their established restaurant. In less than a year the computers, and the Net, have turned their world upside down. For one thing, Rick's is about to become
20 center stage for the home shopping network **QVC**. The cable and on-line network is going to be there showing off **NASCAR** merchandise and its sponsored race car.

Already Rick's has become a **focal point**[5] for local business leaders trying to impress foreign investors. The Denton **Chamber of Commerce**
25 uses the online link at the restaurant to demonstrate how easy it is to work from Denton and still have access to the world.

[1]intrigued = fascinated, interested
[2]digitally = related to computers
[3]espresso = a type of strong coffee
[4]network = computers connected together
[5]focal point = main location

And while the computers are all very impressive, it's not what **lured**[6] me up to Rick's. What caught my attention was all the community information on their Web page.

30   Rather than using its site to push burgers and beer, Rick's has become the Net's window on Denton. There are shopping guides, movie listings, antique shops and community news.

    Some people make it a daily stop to check e-mail. One customer, a roofer, pulls up national weather reports, satellite images of cities **battered**[7]
35 by storms, then maps he and his crew will follow to the location.

    So has it helped business? On the rainy Wednesday after noon I went by, the parking lot was full. By the end of the year, Rick's hopes to expand, adding more tables and, of course, more computers.

    "Rick and I moved here to be part of a community," Teresa says. "We
40 never realized how this would make us such a center of the community."

Source: *The Dallas Morning News*

Check Your Comprehension

1. Who visits Rick's American Cyber Grill?

2. Why did the author visit Rick's?

3. How does the Chamber of Commerce use the link at the restaurant?

4. How do people use the computers at Rick's?

5. How have computers affected business at Rick's?

6. Why haven't cybercafés become popular in other places in Texas?

 **READING**

Find out more about **understanding fact and opinion** by looking in the Reference Guide to Reading Strategies on pages xii–xiv.

Understanding Fact and Opinion

Newspaper articles and other types of writing often include a mixture of facts and opinions. It's important to be able to tell the difference—if you read an opinion and think it's a fact, you might be misled.

    Here are some statements related to the reading. Identify them as facts (**F**) or opinions (**O**). The first one is done for you.

  <u>F</u> **1.** Rick's has become a local gathering place, where the regulars surf the Net.

  _____ **2.** The computers at Rick's are as attractive as the games at Chuck E. Cheese's.

  _____ **3.** Cybercafés haven't caught on in Texas.

  _____ **4.** Rick and Teresa's restaurant is the best in Denton.

[6]lured = attracted, drew
[7]battered = beaten

_____ **5.** It is easy to work from Denton and have access to the rest of the world.

_____ **6.** People on the east and west coasts are "cooler" than people in Denton.

_____ **7.** People of all types come to Rick's to use the Internet.

VOCABULARY
Slang and Colloquial Verb Phrases

Fill in the blanks with the slang and colloquial verb phrases below.

isn't your speed   *catches on*   *turns it upside down*
surfs the Net   *shows off*   *pushes burgers and beer*
is all the rage

1. If someone is too proud, he probably _____ a lot.

2. If you don't like something, then it _____ .

3. In order to find information, John _____ .

4. A good restaurant owner _____ .

5. Going to a cybercafé _____ .

6. The Internet not only changes your life, it _____ .

7. If my idea _____ with the public, I'll be rich.

THINK ABOUT IT

1. Why did the author write this article?

2. What conclusions can you draw about Denton, Texas?

3. Why do you think cybercafés are popular?

SYNTHESIS

Discussion and Debate

1. Are you comfortable with technology, or does it make you nervous? Explain your answer.

2. Imagine you could attend school entirely through a computer. (Actually, this is possible!) Would you enjoy that? Why or why not?

3. Is technology making us lazy? If so, how is it doing so? If not, explain your answer.

4. Think of another question to ask your classmates about the ideas in this chapter.

Writing Topics

1. Look through some magazines that feature computers. In your journal, write about what you saw—what things interested you, what things confused you.

2. Does your school need more access to technology, especially the Internet? If so, write a letter to your school's Dean or President, explaining what you need and why. If not, write a letter to your parents or to a friend, telling them about the access you have to technology at your school.

3. Is technology developing too rapidly? Write an essay in which you argue that technology is a benefit or a harm to society. Use examples in your essay.

On Your Own

1. If there is a cybercafé in your community, visit it and report to your class about the experience. If there isn't, visit a cybercafé site on line. (You might try http://www.cybergrill.com).

2. Find a toystore in your community. Go in and look at some of the electronic games and toys. Are they different from the toys you had when you were a child? Discuss your experience with your classmates.

3. Watch a movie that features technology, such as:

   The Net   *1984*   *2001: A Space Odyssey*   *Sneakers*

   Did you enjoy the film? Report on it to your class.

4. Conduct a survey. Ask ten people which electrical items they own, and which they have used in the last 24 hours. Here are some items to include, but you can add more if you like:

   - telephone
   - fax machine
   - personal computer
   - television
   - VCR
   - video camera

   - Internet
   - cellular phone
   - ATM
   - voice mail system
   - electric typewriter

   Compare the results of your survey with those of your classmates. How do they compare the the chart on page 178?

★★

A L M A N A C   For additional cultural information, refer to the Almanac on pages 217–228. The Almanac contains lists of useful facts, maps, and other information to enhance your learning.

CHAPTER 10

Popular Culture

★★

"High culture" includes such things as paintings, classical music, and ballet. Popular culture includes any other form of entertainment that people enjoy such as movies and rock music. Two other interesting aspects of popular culture in the United States are television and cars.

PART ONE

Television: Tuning In

Although television watching has decreased recently, the average American still watches several hours of television a day. It is no surprise that it continues to be the most influential force in the American household.

Before You Read

A Guide to Television Ratings

TV-Y: Suitable for all children
TV-Y shows are created for a very young audience, including children as young as two. These programs will not frighten younger children.

TV-Y7: Suitable for children seven and older
TV-Y7 shows are better for older children who can tell between make-believe and reality. They may include mild physical or comical violence, which may scare children under seven years old.

TV-G: Suitable for a general audience
Although TV-G shows are not made especially for children, they contain little or no violence, no strong language and little or no sexual content. Many parents will find these shows okay for their kids.

TV-PG: Parental guidance suggested
TV-PG shows may contain material that some parents will not want their younger children to see. Such programs may contain some swearing, a little violence, or scenes where the actors talk about sex.

TV-14: May be unsuitable for children under 14
TV-14 programs may contain complicated topics, sexual content, strong language and violence. Parents are strongly warned that they may find such programs unsuitable for children under age 14.

TV-M: For mature audiences only
TV-M programs are designed to be viewed by adults only. Such programs may contain mature topics, swearing, graphic violence, and sex.

Look at the list of ratings and discuss these questions with classmates:

- Do the categories of television shows on the list make sense? How would you change the categories?
- Do you think this kind of list helps parents control what their children watch?
- Do you check the television rating on a show before you watch it?

Cultural Cues

ABC, NBC, CBS, Fox The four major television networks in the United States.

JANUARY 17, 1997 Ratings War

Do the new TV ratings tell parents what they really need to know?

Annie Suzak's mom and dad now have an answer to the question they love to ask when
5 Annie watches TV. "My parents always ask, 'Is that show for kids?' " says Annie, 13, of Oak Park, Illinois. "With the ratings, they can make sure I'm not lying."

Last week network TV got a new ratings
10 system to keep kids honest and parents informed. Shows on **ABC, NBC, CBS** and **Fox** are now **tagged with**[1] coded ratings intended to help parents decide what kids should watch. All channels should carry ratings by the end of
15 January.

The codes appear in the upper-left-hand corner of the TV screen for the first 15 seconds of a 30-minute show. They are similar to movie ratings (see chart). "We wanted to keep it as
20 simple as possible," says Barbara Dixon, spokesperson for the group that invented the new system. Parents already know movie ratings, Dixon said, so the group felt that a similar system would work best.

25 A happy ending? Not so fast

Not everyone agrees. The PTA, **pediatricians**[2], church groups and others claim the new ratings don't give parents enough information. For instance, a show may be rated TV-14 be-
30 cause of nasty words, violence or **racy**[3] love scenes, or perhaps all three. Critics of the new

system want the ratings to **specify**[4] the reasons for the rating. One idea is to add a "V" for violence, an "S" for sex and so forth. "Tell par-
35 ents what's in the show, and let them decide what is appropriate for their kids," says Vicky Rideout of Children Now in Oakland, California.

Many opponents of the new ratings system
40 suspect that TV producers don't want ratings to be specific because that could scare off advertisers. "The producers' main **motive**[5] is to sell TV time to advertisers," says Donald K. Freedheim of the American Psychological As-
45 sociation, which opposes the ratings. Companies may not want their ads to run during shows with adults-only ratings.

This is only a test

The ratings war really started with a new
50 law passed last February. By 1998, according to the law, all new TVs must be made with a V-chip. This tiny computer chip will enable parents to block out shows with certain ratings. After the law was passed, President Clinton
55 met with bosses from the TV industry. The producers promised to come up with a fair system of rating their own TV shows and to test it for 10 months before starting to use it with the new V-chip televisions.
60 President Clinton did not applaud or attack the new system when it was announced last month. "We might be able to make it better," he said. "The parents' groups, the **advocacy**[6]

---

[1]tagged with = labeled, given labels
[2]pediatricians = children's doctors
[3]racy = sexy

[4]specify = name specifically
[5]motive = purpose
[6]advocacy = support

groups deserve to be heard and considered.
65 But we are now doing what I think ought to be done."

What do kids think?

Kids are just beginning to notice the new ratings. Colin Wilson, a ninth-grader in Fort
70 Worth, Texas, says they won't change what he watches. He often gets to pick his own shows. "I trust his judgment," says his mom, Claudia Wilson. "The ratings system may be helpful to some people, but basic common sense works
75 equally well."

Stephen Barnes, 12, of Brooklyn, New York, thinks a TV-M rating might tempt kids who are flipping channels. But what kids see in movies and video games is often more violent or
80 grownup than TV shows, he says. "Most parents don't know what their kids watch, anyway."

Fans and **foes**[7] of the new system agree on one thing: no system will work unless parents get involved. Some parents have already laid
85 down new rules.

"I'm allowed to watch G and PG shows by myself," says Eric Fowler, 9, of McLean, Virginia. "But shows that are TV-14, I have to watch with my mom and dad."

Source: *Time For Kids*

[7]foes = enemies

Check Your Comprehension

1. How does the new ratings system work?
2. Who is Barbara Dixon?
3. Why do some groups disagree with the ratings system?
4. Why do the opponents think that the TV ratings aren't specific enough?
5. What is a V-chip? What does it do?
6. Did President Clinton support the new system?
7. How do kids feel about the system?
8. What is one thing that both the supporters and opponents of the system agree on?

READING

Find out more about **summarizing** by looking in the Reference Guide to Reading Strategies on pages xii–xiv.

Summarizing

Use the following space to write a short summary of the article.
Then compare your summary to a classmate's. How are they different? What would you change in yours?

VOCABULARY
Using Prepositions

Refer to the reading to see how these prepositions are used. Write the correct preposition in the blanks. You may use the prepositions more than once.

by	*for*	*of*
off	*on*	*with*

1. Is that show _____ kids?

2. _____ the ratings, they can make sure I'm not lying.

3. Shows _____ ABC, NBC, CBS and Fox now have ratings.

4. All channels will carry ratings _____ the end _____ January.

5. The codes appear _____ the first 15 seconds _____ a 30-minute show.

6. Barbara Dixon is the spokesperson _____ the group that invented the new system.

7. A show may be rated TV-14 because _____ nasty words.

8. One idea is to add a "V" _____ violence.

9. Ratings could scare _____ advertisers.

10. All new televisions must be made _____ a V-chip

THINK ABOUT IT

1. What is your opinion of the ratings system? Will it work?

2. Do you think children should not watch violence on television?

3. What was your favorite television show as a child? What rating do you think it would receive today?

4. Does your country provide ratings for television programs? What is programming like for children in your country?

Before You Read

Oprah Winfrey

Biography

Occupation: TV Personality, Producer, Actress

Birthdate: January 29, 1954

Birthplace: Kosciusko, Mississippi, United States

Education: Tennessee State University

This article discusses the success of a very famous American television personality, Oprah Winfrey.

Before you read, think about the following questions:

- Have you ever seen the Oprah Winfrey show?
- Do you like talk shows on television?

READING

Find out more about **skimming** by looking in the Reference Guide to Reading Strategies on pages xii–xiv.

Skimming

Remember that skimming means reading something quickly to get the main idea. Read the article quickly—take no more than three minutes. Then answer these questions:

1. What is important about Oprah Winfrey? _____

_____

2. What was Oprah's early life like? _____

_____

3. What does Oprah struggle with in her personal life? _____

_____

Now, read the story more carefully.

Cultural Cues

Forbes A magazine focusing on financial stories and advice.

Steven Spielberg A successful film director; his films include *E.T., the Extra-Terrestrial, Close Encounters of the Third Kind, The Color Purple, Schindler's List,* and *Amistad.*

Alice Walker An American writer whose most famous work is *The Color Purple.*

Mary Pickford An American actor from the early part of the century.

Lucille Ball An American comedian popular in the 1950s and 1960s; her most famous show was *I Love Lucy.*

Queen of Talk and More

by Ian Hodder

"All my life I have always known I was born to greatness."
—Oprah Winfrey

The reigning queen of all media is talk-show host Oprah Winfrey. Her influence goes beyond her daily one-hour show into everything from the publishing business to the agricultural mar-
5 kets. Do you need proof? When Winfrey discusses an unknown author on her show, his book goes to the top of the best-seller charts. She cleverly renegotiates her contract, and **Forbes** soon calls her the world's highest-
10 paid entertainer. She starts a new exercise program, and thousands of people adopt her regimen. She establishes a television and film studio in West Chicago, and the formerly troubled neighborhood undergoes an eco-
15 nomic rebirth. She discusses mad cow disease on her show, and American cattle markets suffer. Yet, regardless of how great her authority becomes, Oprah remains the plain speaking, empathetic best girlfriend to American
20 homemakers.

Even occasional viewers of *The Oprah Winfrey Show* know about its host's troubled childhood. She was born to unwed teenage parents in rural Mississippi. She spent her childhood
25 living in extreme poverty on her grandmother's farm. (Incidentally, "Oprah" is an accidental misspelling of the biblical name Orpah.) She moved to Milwaukee as a **preteen**[1] to live with her mother, Vernita Lee, under whose roof she
30 was sexually molested by male relatives. Winfrey spent her early teens in and out of trouble. At age fourteen, she gave birth to a **premature**[2] baby, who died shortly thereafter. Facing the threat of being sent to a home for troubled
35 youth, Winfrey went to live with her father in Nashville. Vernon Winfrey, a barber and businessman, provided the discipline that was lacking in his daughter's life. He instituted a strict curfew and stressed the value of education,
40 and under his iron fist, Oprah turned her life around quickly.

At age nineteen, Winfrey got her first broadcasting job. She was a reporter at radio station WVOL in Nashville. She also enrolled at Ten-
45 nessee State University to study speech and performing arts. In her sophomore year, 1972, Winfrey switched interests and became the first African-American television news **anchor**[3] in Nashville. She moved to Baltimore in

[1]preteen = before the age of 13

[2]premature = born before 9 months

[3]anchor = main news reporter on television

50 1976 and, after two years working as a reporter and co-anchor, she was hired to host the station's talk show, *People Are Talking*. At first, the management didn't quite know what to think of Winfrey—a black, overweight woman
55 working in a white man's appearance-**obsessed**[4] world. Viewers, however, responded very well to her. In 1984, after eight years in Baltimore, Winfrey nervously accepted a job as host of *A.M. Chicago*, a morning show.
60 She had reason to be nervous: the program was scheduled opposite Phil Donahue's top-rated national talk show.

It turned out that her worries were unfounded. Within months, Winfrey's *A.M. Chi-*
65 *cago* was beating its rival. Rather than try to imitate Donahue, Winfrey simply was herself. "The closest thing that Phil Donahue ever talked about was the fact that he was a **wayward**[5] Catholic. Other than that, talk show
70 hosts didn't talk about themselves," explained the talk-show host Maury Povich in an interview with *Working Woman* magazine. "Oprah opened up a lot of new windows because they could empathize with her." Winfrey, who had
75 always wanted to be an actress but had no professional experience, then landed a good movie role playing Sofia in **Steven Spielberg**'s 1985 adaptation of **Alice Walker**'s *The Color Purple*. For her performance, Winfrey received
80 an Oscar nomination for Best Supporting Actress.

The good publicity that came with her nomination couldn't have come at a better time. Winfrey was scheduled to do her program—
85 now titled *The Oprah Winfrey Show*—as a national program, in 1986. The change to a large audience went well, and the top-rated Donahue now found himself competing with Oprah. During this period of **expansion**[6], Winfrey began
90 giving herself a large part of her show's profits. She established Harpo Productions ("Harpo"

is Oprah spelled backwards). Oprah Winfrey is the third woman in history—after **Mary Pickford** and **Lucille Ball**—to own a major studio,
95 and is well on her way to becoming the first African-American billionaire (she earned an estimated $97 million in 1996).

In 1994, with her fortieth birthday fast approaching, Winfrey found herself at both a per-
100 sonal and professional crossroads. Daytime television had become crowded with **chitchat**[7]. Winfrey and her many competitors offered topics that appealed to audiences who liked gossip and scandal. Even though Winfrey
105 remained the leader of the talk show genre, talk-TV had turned terribly trashy. The thought of retiring from the show to concentrate on acting and producing occurred to Winfrey often. But instead of leaving the show, Winfrey
110 promised to refocus her show on uplifting, meaningful subjects. She believed that her audience would stick with her even if her show's topics were less **sensationalistic**[8]. Because of Winfrey's promise, the past few years of "The
115 Oprah Winfrey Show" have featured fewer pornographers and prostitutes, and far more poetry and **pop psychology**[9]. Despite an early drop in ratings, Winfrey's popularity is now as strong as ever.

120 In spite of her success, Winfrey has had an ongoing battle with her weight. After weighing around two hundred pounds from 1984 to 1987, the five-foot-seven hostess lost sixty-seven pounds on a liquid diet and showed off her thin
125 figure in 1989. Within a year, she regained the weight, plus an additional three pounds. In 1991, Winfrey hired chef Rosie Daley to cook low-fat food. The following year, exercise specialist Bob Greene became Winfrey's personal
130 trainer. Almost ninety pounds melted away thanks to Daley's fat-free food and Greene's difficult daily workouts. In 1995, a thin Winfrey competed in a marathon and finished with a

---

[4]obsessed = fanatical, extremely focused

[5]wayward = not following the rules

[6]expansion = growth

[7]chitchat = light talk

[8]sensationalistic = getting a lot of attention

[9]pop psychology = popular psychology

good time. Her TV audience witnessed the
135 transformation first-hand, and, when Daley and
Greene each published Winfrey-related books,
they became bestsellers.

Winfrey's spare time is spent with her fiancé
Stedman Graham, a public relations executive.
140 She also has a beloved **cocker spaniel**[10], Solo-

mon. The couple (and dog) reside primarily in
a penthouse condominium overlooking Lake
Michigan, and they take vacations at Winfrey's
property in Rolling Prairie, Indiana, or at her
145 85-acre ranch near Telluride, Colorado.

---

[10]cocker spaniel = a type of dog

Source: www.celebsite.com

Check Your Comprehension

1. Besides her talk show, what other professional activities does Oprah participate in?

2. What was Oprah's childhood like?

3. Why was Oprah nervous when she first began her talk show in Chicago?

4. Who is Phil Donahue?

5. What has been Oprah's biggest challenge?

6. How did Oprah get into shape?

7. How has Oprah's show changed since its beginning?

8. How did Oprah affect the cattle industry?

VOCABULARY
No Dictionary!

Do you know these words? Find them in the reading, and try to determine what they mean from context. Don't use your dictionary!

1. crossroads _____

2. curfew _____

3. empathetic _____

4. genre _____

5. marathon _____

6. penthouse _____

7. regimen _____

8. reign _____

9. renegotiate _____

10. scandal _____

THINK ABOUT IT

1. How is Oprah's life history a "typical American story"?

2. Oprah's influence continues to grow. She has recently started a book club. She recommends a book, and then it is discussed on her television show. When Oprah recommends a book, it quickly goes to the top of the bestseller list.

   Here are some of the books she has recommended:

   The Rapture of Canaan by Sheri Reynolds

   Stones From the River by Ursula Hegi

   She's Come Undone by Wally Lamb

   The Deep End of the Ocean by Jacquelyn Mitchard

   Song of Solomon by Toni Morrison

   The Book of Ruth by Jane Hamilton

   Have you heard of any of these books? Would you read a book that was recommended by a television host? Why or why not?

3. Why do you think people enjoy talk shows? Look in a current television listing to see how many there are. Does this number surprise you?

PART TWO

Cars: Driving Passions

The American love affair with the automobile is well-known. In this part of the chapter, you will read about how a car can sometimes become an object of love and sometimes a dangerous weapon.

Before You Read

Getting a car is often an important rite of passage in an American teenager's life. In this article, the author talks about his first car.

Before you read this story, think about the following questions:

- Have you ever owned a car? When did you buy your first one?
- Why do you think some people are sentimental about their first car?

About the Author   Lou Ross was once the Vice Chairman of the Ford Automobile Corporation.

by Lou Ross   My **First** Car

Do you know what happens when a car is too old to run anymore?

Someone sells it to a teenager, and for a few brief months at the end of a long life of
5 service that old machine becomes newer than new again, an aged teacher of new freedoms, and the taskmaster of all the responsibilities that come with them.

That's the way it was with my first car. It
10 was a 13-year-old 1937 Plymouth with a **bumper**[1] held on with **baling wire**[2], a **clutch**[3] that scraped like chalk against a blackboard, and an inability to go to bed at night without first being tucked in.

15 That's right. It had to be tucked in at night. That's because it was more than a little sensitive to night dew, or rain, or anything that felt like moisture. It made a pretty good **barometer**[4], now that I think on it, for it would tell
20 you when it was going to rain by a complete refusal to start.

As an **ingenious**[5] engineer in the making (the older you get, the more ingenious you remember you were when you were young), I
25 carried a blanket and a surplus army **poncho**[6] to cover up the hood every night.

That old car got to liking being tucked in, and toward the end, I had to cover the **hood**[7] every night. Most nights that worked, but when
30 it didn't, well, a '37 Plymouth is light enough

to get a friend, sometimes, my wife-to-be Carolyn, to push the car by hand to get it started.

The memories that surround that car still start up for me a lot better than that Plymouth
35 ever did.

Mostly, they are the remembrances of paying for the car—the total price of $75, insurance, repairs, and operating costs. And they include the memories of how the car paid me
40 back with interest.

I was 18 years old and a freshman at Wayne State University. I was the first one ever in my family to go to college, so the family was proud; but my father was a Detroit City policeman,
45 and with two other kids at home, there wasn't any budget for college tuition, books, and least of all, anything as frivolous as the purchase of a car.

Yet then, as now, a car seemed like a practi-
50 cal necessity. I had to get up at 6 A.M. to ride the city bus in order to get to class by 8 A.M. A car could save me hours every day, and give me the flexibility to take on additional weekend odd jobs.

55 So when I took my first summer job at "Ford's," in the Dearborn Assembly Plant, getting a car was a wish, tucked just behind the demand of earning my fall tuition.

Not only did I earn the money that summer,
60 but I learned a respect for assembly work that I carry with me to this day.

For my job on the line was to guide the front end sheet metal down onto the moving **chassis-body**[8] **conveyor**[9]. Then I had to drop
65 to my knees onto the **corrugated**[10] surface of

---

[1]bumper = part of a car body

[2]baling wire = wire used to hold bales of hay together.

[3]clutch = part of a car's engine

[4]barometer = instrument that measures air pressure

[5]ingenious = very smart, clever

[6]poncho = a type of cape used to keep off rain

[7]hood = the part of the car body covering the engine

[8]chassis = the frame of a car

[9]conveyor = type of belt that moves parts in a factory

[10]corrugated = having a wavy surface

the conveyor line, and wrestle a three-inch bolt through a frame bracket, add a one-inch chunk of rubber, two inches of spring to compress, and thread it into the radiator support. Well, I
70 had been a varsity football and baseball player in high school, and that job took every bit of my physical endurance and more to survive.

In later years, I helped my two sons find work in Ford plants so they could gain the
75 appreciation for plant life and develop a sincere **conviction**[11] **engendered**[12] by hard work, to complete their college education.

At summer's end, I was back on the city bus **en route**[13] to school when we passed a
80 1937 Plymouth on the street with a sign in the window—"For Sale. $75.00." I got off the bus and bought it immediately.

That was my first mistake, for I hadn't gotten my father involved in the decision or even
85 asked for advice in advance. He probably felt a little cheated, and was upset, especially since the car needed a new clutch that he could have warned me about. But my dad accepted my apologies and the **inevitability**[14] of the deci-

90 sion, and he even paid for a new clutch out of his pocket.

For six months I got to school in that car, and saved an hour-and-a-half a day, as I anticipated. Much of that time, however, was in-
95 vested in keeping it running, becoming truly intimate with the Plymouth under the hood. And, there were a few minutes every night when I tucked it in with blanket and poncho.

The car actually paid for itself. For I was
100 at Carolyn's house one day when a TV repair truck backed into the parked Plymouth and damaged the bumper, or what was left of the bumper. The insurance company paid me $75, which was the original price of the car. Of
105 course, I kept on driving the car with the dangling bumper, and a couple of years later **scrapped it out**[15] for $25.

All experiences eventually end up in scrapbooks, and that's literally true of your first car.
110 Yet there will always be a clear picture of that '37 Plymouth, and what it taught me, in my mind. You don't forget a car you have to tuck in bed every night.

[11]conviction = dedication

[12]engendered = created

[13]en route = on the way

[14]inevitability = fate, unavoidable nature

Source: www.speechwriting.com

[15]scrapped it out = sold it for scrap metal

Check Your Comprehension

1. What condition was the car in when Mr. Ross bought it?

2. What mistake did he make when he first bought it?

3. How did the car get damaged?

4. How did the car change Mr. Ross's life?

5. What does he mean that he had to "tuck the car in" at night?

6. How did the car "pay for itself"?

7. Why did he buy the car?

READING

Find out more about **reading graphics and statistics** by looking in the Reference Guide to Reading Strategies on pages xii–xiv.

Reading Graphics and Statistics

Look at the following table, then answer the questions that follow it.

Automobile Statistics for Selected States

State	Percentage of population who are licensed drivers	Drivers per car	Gallons of fuel used per car	Average miles per gallon	Annual miles driven per car
Alaska	71.9	.82	569	13.66	7,779
California	64.1	.90	670	18.17	12,174
Florida	78.9	1.07	713	16.69	11,899
Hawaii	63.2	.96	535	19.04	10,188
Massachusetts	74.0	1.11	667	17.49	11,669
Michigan	69.5	.87	675	16.66	11,247
Montana	61.4	.55	633	15.16	9,601
New York	57.1	1.02	616	17.98	11,080
Texas	65.9	.89	762	17.17	13,089
Wyoming	71.8	.67	995	13.20	13,137
Average for the United States	67.4	.89	707	16.84	11,916

1. In which state do people drive the least? _____

2. In which state do people drive the most? _____

3. Which states are below the national average for total fuel consumption? _____

4. Which states are above the national average for average miles per gallon? _____

5. Which state has the most drivers per car? _____

6. What two states are most similar in their driving habits? _____

7. How did you decide your answer for number 6? _____

VOCABULARY
Car Terminology

In this reading, several words for parts of cars were introduced. In the following drawing, label the parts of the car listed.

radiator	*hubcap*
clutch	*steering wheel*
bumper	*trunk*
hood	*brake*
windshield	*accelerator*

THINK ABOUT IT

1. In your opinion, why did the author write this essay?

2. Why do people grow fond of their cars?

3. Cars are one of the major sources of environmental damage. Should people drive less? How else can we protect the environment against automobile pollution?

Before You Read

Improper Driving Reported in Accidents

Type of driving	Percentage of fatal accidents	Percentage of injury accidents	Percentage of all accidents
Improper driving	68.1	73.5	75.5
Speed too fast or unsafe	19.8	13.9	14.0
Right of way	15.2	25.5	22.9
—failed to yield	10.2	18.1	17.0
—passed stop sign	3.0	5.0	4.0
—ignored signal	2.2	2.4	1.9
Drove left of center line	9.1	2.4	2.2
Improper passing	1.5	1.3	1.5
Made improper turn	2.3	2.8	4.2
Followed too closely	0.5	7.0	7.2
Other improper driving	19.7	20.7	23.6
No improper driving stated	31.9	26.5	24.5

 Watch the CNN video on fixing old cars. Discuss these questions:

1. What kind of cars do the men work on?

2. Why do they choose this kind of car?

3. How do people act when they see these cars on the road?

U.S. roads are becoming more crowded, and some people would argue that driving is getting more difficult. In this article, the author writes about "road rage," acts of anger that often result in accidents.

Before you read, discuss these questions with classmates:

• Describe each type of improper driving in the chart. Which ones have you been guilty of?

• Do you think drivers are becoming ruder?

• Have you seen an automobile accident? What do you think caused it?

Cultural Cues

NPR National Public Radio, a publicly-funded radio program.

AAA The Automobile Association of America, a club that supplies maps and road service to its members.

Fourth Amendment The Fourth Amendment of the U.S. Constitution, which protects citizens from illegal police searches.

About the Author

Csaba Csere writes for *Car and Driver* magazine.

by Csaba Csere Road Rage

Last July, on **NPR,** I heard Dr. Ricardo Martinez, the head of the National Highway Traffic Safety Administration [NHTSA], state that "aggressive drivers" account for 28,000 traffic
5 deaths per year. That is about two-thirds of the 41,907 traffic fatalities that were recorded for 1996. This made me think. NHTSA has been saying for years that drunk drivers account for half of traffic deaths and speeders for another
10 third. And what about fatal accidents caused by bad weather, road **hazards**[1], mechanical failures, and drivers falling asleep at the wheel, talking on cellular phones, or simply making mistakes? It seems like there aren't enough
15 traffic **fatalities**[2] to account for all these causes.

There's no need for a Congressional investigation. Dr. Martinez had already been to the capitol to explain. He defined aggressive driv-
20 ers as individuals who are more likely to: "speed, tailgate, fail to yield, weave in and out of traffic, pass on the right, make improper and unsafe lane changes, run stop signs and red lights, make hand and facial gestures, scream,
25 honk, flash their lights, be **impaired**[3] by alcohol or drugs, drive unbelted, or take other unsafe actions." Given the inclusiveness of this list, whatever could possibly cause the 13,000 or so traffic deaths that Dr. Martinez does not
30 attribute to aggressive drivers?

Dr. Martinez went on to explain that these "aggressive" drivers are possibly suffering from "stress disorders that lead to impaired judgment." He sees three factors linked to aggres-
35 sive driving: 1. lack of responsible driving behavior, 2. reduced levels of traffic enforcement, 3. increased congestion and travel in urban areas.

But what really causes this new social prob-
40 lem? The government has a long history of allocating millions to investigate why people commit crimes or fail to escape poverty. Where is NHTSA's search for the root causes of this so-called road rage?

45 One organization that has explored this issue is the **AAA** Foundation for Traffic Safety [FTS]. In three studies published last March, the AAA FTS estimated that road rage kills or injures at least 1,500 people each year. As
50 terrible as that is, this is much lower than Dr. Martinez's figures. But then, these studies defined aggressive driving as "an angry or impatient motorist or passenger who injures or kills another motorist, passenger, or pedestrian, in
55 response to a traffic **dispute**[4], **altercation**[5], or **grievance**[6]." I think everyone would agree that such acts are truly road-rageous.

What's interesting is that while the studies find many motivations for drivers to become
60 angry, the No. 1 cause is lane blocking. Next come tailgating and changing lanes without using turn signals. Although no one would suggest that such motoring **misdemeanors**[7] justify **vehicular homicide,**[8] they do indicate
65 that we could reduce these incidents if drivers followed the rules of the road.

[1]hazards = dangers
[2]fatalities = deaths
[3]impaired = unable to perform well
[4]dispute = argument
[5]altercation = fight
[6]grievance = complaint
[7]misdemeanors = small crimes
[8]vehicular homicide = killing someone with a car

Unfortunately, knowledge of these rules seems to be dropping fast. More and more school districts have removed driver training from their programs. Even the Los Angeles Unified School District, which serves students in the nation's most auto-dependent city, has eliminated driver education.

Education is one of the solutions that Dr. Martinez proposed, but he didn't suggest improving driver education. NHTSA is sending out tip sheets to "highway safety professionals and **advocates**[9]" and promoting a nationwide cell-phone number to report incidents of aggressive driving. Aggressive driving, as he defined it, includes almost all vehicular **infractions**[10], real or imagined.

The safety agency has also "distributed public information and education materials on aggressive driving to the 23 major media markets." This perhaps accounts for the recent flurry of sensationalist stories on the various TV **quasi-news**[11] magazines. ABC recently reran a "Primetime Live" story in which Sam Donaldson arranged to clog the left lane of the Washington Beltway during rush hour in a camera van driving at 55 mph. He then went into his trademark annoying ignorant act when drivers expressed irritation, occasionally with universally understood gestures, that some **blockhead**[12] in a blocky vehicle was blocking the passing lane. This is education?

Dr. Martinez also proposes more **vigorous**[13] law enforcement against "aggressive drivers" and is organizing **crackdowns**[14] in various states. As part of this program, he would like to install automated-laser-imaging and video-speed-detection devices and high-resolution traffic cameras. So much for the **Fourth Amendment** protecting us from unreasonable search and seizure. However, if an **impartial**[15] committee of citizens could scan the tapes for evidence of government officials in various acts of financial or personal misconduct, it might be worth it.

These proposed solutions suggest that this entire "aggressive driving" campaign is simply a new public-relations game. It is designed to **prosecute**[16] and **persecute**[17] NHTSA's usual suspects, now that the old slogans no longer work. "Speed kills," for example, has become difficult to sell since NHTSA has been forced to admit that traffic deaths in 1996 increased only 0.25 percent after 24 states increased their highway speed limits.

It is good, however, to see NHTSA talking more about crash avoidance than crash survival. However, with the dangers of **airbags**[18] more in the news than their benefits, perhaps it was inevitable.

Further evidence of this shift comes from NHTSA's "Crashes Aren't Accidents" campaign that began last December. In this campaign, Dr. Martinez told his staff "to eliminate the word *accident* from the field of unintentional injury." He described motor vehicle crashes as "predictable, preventable events. We can identify their causes and prevent them."

We couldn't agree more, but simply blaming every driver who has ever flashed a headlight at a road hog or **banishing**[19] the word *accident* from the dictionary will not, by themselves, eliminate a single car crash.

Source: *Car and Driver* Magazine

[9]advocates = supporters

[10]infractions = violations of the laws

[11]quasi-news = something like news, not exactly news

[12]blockhead = stupid person

[13]vigorous = strong

[14]crackdowns = extra enforcement of the rules

[15]impartial = not favoring one side or another

[16]prosecute = sue in court

[17]persecute = oppress

[18]airbags = safety devices

[19]banishing = eliminating

Check Your Comprehension

1. Why did the author question the statistics about traffic fatalities?

2. What is wrong with the NHTSA's definition of "aggressive drivers," according to the author?

3. What is the main reason drivers get angry, according to the reading?

4. What effect did higher speed limits have on traffic deaths?

5. What is the author's point of view about "road rage"?

 READING

Find out more about **understanding the main idea** by looking in the Reference Guide to Reading Strategies on pages xii–xiv.

Understanding the Main Idea

The author proposed several ideas in his article. What are they? How does he support them? Fill out the following table. The first example is done for you.

Idea	Support
1. The NHTSA has inflated its statistics about road rage.	The numbers don't add up; there aren't enough fatalities to account for their percentages.
2.	
3.	
4.	
5.	

VOCABULARY
Using New Vocabulary

This reading has a lot of words that might have been new to you. Look at the following list of words. Draw a line to each word's closest match. Refer to the reading if you need help.

1. *airbag*		argument
2. *altercation*		death
3. *an advocate*		sue in court
4. *banishing*		not favoring one side or another
5. *blockhead*		stupid person
6. *crackdown*		oppress
7. *fatality*		eliminating
8. *grievance*		danger
9. *hazard*		killing someone with a car
10. *impaired*		safety device
11. *impartial*		fight
12. *infraction*		strong
13. *misdemeanor*		violation of the laws
14. *persecute*		extra enforcement of the rules
15. *prosecute*		unable to perform well
16. *vehicular homicide*		supporter
17. *vigorous*		small crime

THINK ABOUT IT

1. Do you agree with the author's point of view about road rage? Why or why not?

2. There have been recent proposals to raise the age limit for drivers to 18 from 16, which it is in most states. What do you think of this proposal?

3. The author points out that driver's education classes are being cut at many high schools. Do you think these classes should be kept? Why or why not?

S Y N T H E S I S

Discussion and Debate

1. Cars and television are two important parts of American life. Some would even say that these items are essential parts of the American lifestyle. What other items are important to the American lifestyle, in your opinion?

2. Some scholars say that material possessions are a reflection of a particular value in a society. For example, automobiles might be a symbol of Americans' love of independence and movement. Make a list of other possessions or activities that are important to Americans and discuss what values you think they might represent.

3. How are attitudes towards cars different in the United States than in your country? Are attitudes toward television different? In what way?

4. Think of another question to ask your classmates about the ideas in this chapter.

Writing Topics

1. In your journal, write about a television personality or program that has had an influence on your life. What makes that show or person so special to you?

2. What kind of car would you like to own? Write a short essay describing the car of your dreams. Use plenty of detail.

3. Choose one of the following topics and write an essay in which you argue your point of view:
   a. Cars are a necessary and enjoyable part of life.
   b. Cars cause damage to the environment; we should change our driving habits.
   c. Television has a negative influence on children.
   d. Television is an important form of entertainment; it provides comfort and amusement to people.

On Your Own

1. Look at recent television listings. What kinds of shows seem to be most popular? Watch a popular television show and discuss it with your class.

2. Find some car advertisements for different kinds of cars. Look carefully at the ads: who are they advertising to? How do you know that? Discuss these ads with your class.

3. Many television shows and films have cars as a main focus. Watch one of the following films or television shows (in reruns, if they're available). Talk about what you saw with your class.

   My Mother the Car (television)

   Herbie the Love Bug (television)

   The Love Bug (film)

Knight Rider (television)
American Graffiti (film)
Corvette Summer (film)
Ferris Bueller's Day Off (film)

★★★

A L M A N A C For additional cultural information, refer to the Almanac on pages 217–228. The Almanac contains lists of useful facts, maps, and other information to enhance your learning.

★★★

1. Map of the United States showing state capitals

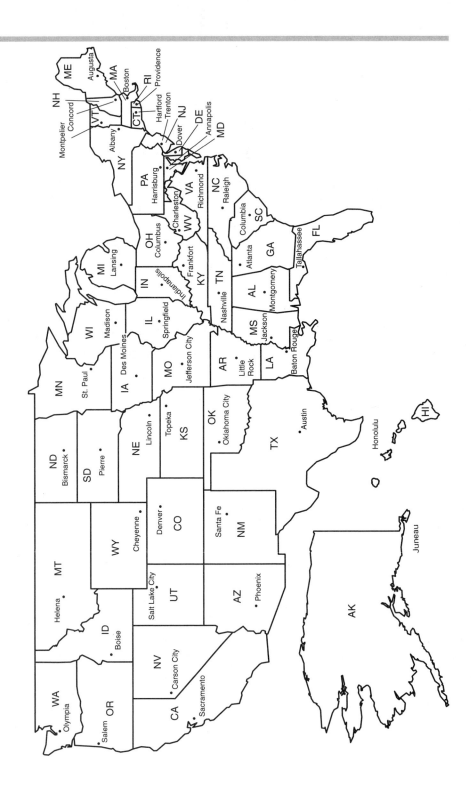

2. Geographic Map of the United States

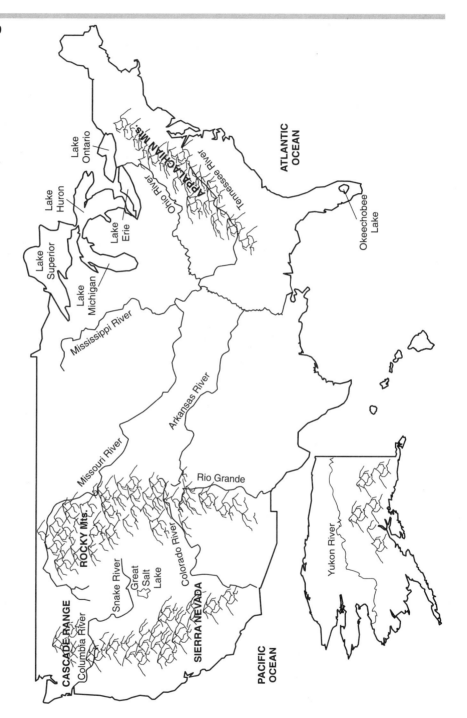

3. Total Population of the States in the United States

	Latest estimate
UNITED STATES	248,709,873
ALABAMA	4,040,587
ARKANSAS	550,043
ARIZONA	3,665,228
ARKANSAS	2,350,725
CALIFORNIA	29,760,021
COLORADO	3,294,394
CONNECTICUT	3,287,116
DELAWARE	666,168
DISTRICT OF COLUMBIA	606,900
FLORIDA	12,937,926
GEORGIA	6,478,216
HAWAII	1,108,229
IDAHO	1,006,749
ILLINOIS	11,430,602
INDIANA	5,544,159
IOWA	2,776,755
KANSAS	2,477,574
KENTUCKY	3,685,296
LOUISIANA	4,219,973
MAINE	1,227,928
MARYLAND	4,781,468
MASSACHUSETTS	6,016,425
MICHIGAN	9,295,297
MINNESOTA	4,375,099
MISSISSIPPI	2,573,216
MISSOURI	5,117,073
MONTANA	799,065
NEBRASKA	1,578,385
NEVADA	1,201,833
NEW HAMPSHIRE	1,109,252
NEW JERSEY	7,730,188
NEW MEXICO	1,515,069
NEW YORK	17,990,455
NORTH CAROLINA	6,628,637
NORTH DAKOTA	638,800
OHIO	10,847,115
OKLAHOMA	3,145,585
OREGON	2,842,321
PENNSYLVANIA	11,881,643
RHODE ISLAND	1,003,464
SOUTH CAROLINA	3,486,703
SOUTH DAKOTA	696,004
TENNESSEE	4,877,185
TEXAS	16,986,510
UTAH	1,722,850
VERMONT	562,758
VIRGINIA	6,187,358
WASHINGTON	4,866,692
WEST VIRGINIA	1,793,477
WISCONSIN	4,891,769
WYOMING	453,588

Source: Population Estimates Branch, U.S. Bureau of the Census, Release date: Aug. 1996

4. Population of the States in the United States by Ethnic Background

	Total	Total Hispanic	White Total	White Hispanic	White non-Hispanic	Black	American Indian	Asian & Pacific Islander
UNITED STATES	265,283,783	28,268,895	219,748,786	25,771,113	193,977,673	33,503,435	2,288,119	9,743,443
ALABAMA	4,273,084	35,857	3,125,926	30,401	3,095,525	1,103,986	15,385	27,787
ALASKA	607,007	22,356	462,255	18,075	444,180	23,325	95,339	26,088
ARIZONA	4,428,068	941,479	3,936,621	880,294	3,056,327	153,888	248,490	89,069
ARKANSAS	2,509,793	40,852	2,076,142	36,088	2,040,054	403,466	13,170	17,015
CALIFORNIA	31,878,234	9,630,188	25,491,661	9,011,827	16,479,834	2,371,293	303,494	3,711,786
COLORADO	3,822,676	535,917	3,535,813	503,635	3,032,178	164,343	35,538	86,982
CONNECTICUT	3,274,238	253,245	2,895,483	223,705	2,671,778	297,984	7,906	72,865
DELAWARE	724,842	22,774	572,853	19,365	553,488	136,062	2,434	13,493
DISTRICT OF CO-LUMBIA	543,213	37,705	184,638	30,035	154,603	340,837	1,692	16,046
FLORIDA	14,399,985	2,022,110	11,930,830	1,879,468	10,051,362	2,172,252	51,592	245,311
GEORGIA	7,353,225	187,392	5,130,880	163,122	4,967,758	2,074,548	17,086	130,711
HAWAII	1,183,723	93,100	395,969	46,444	349,525	35,514	6,515	745,725
IDAHO	1,189,251	80,976	1,154,199	75,050	1,079,149	6,438	15,856	12,758
ILLINOIS	11,846,544	1,136,282	9,639,662	1,063,265	8,576,397	1,806,901	26,210	373,771
INDIANA	5,840,528	129,277	5,297,205	118,023	5,179,182	477,928	14,022	51,373
IOWA	2,851,792	49,865	2,754,355	45,164	2,709,191	55,047	8,358	34,032
KANSAS	2,572,150	124,842	2,355,375	112,989	2,242,386	152,166	22,903	41,706
KENTUCKY	3,883,723	28,543	3,573,069	24,406	3,548,663	279,930	5,891	24,833
LOUISIANA	4,350,579	109,969	2,884,225	94,301	2,789,924	1,393,678	19,346	53,330
MAINE	1,243,316	8,446	1,223,690	7,598	1,216,092	5,729	5,578	8,319
MARYLAND	5,071,604	170,052	3,494,905	141,828	3,353,077	1,373,129	15,343	188,227
MASSACHU-SETTS	6,092,352	348,181	5,499,644	275,693	5,223,951	377,715	14,279	200,714
MICHIGAN	9,594,350	242,128	8,024,496	215,033	7,809,463	1,368,804	58,939	142,111
MINNESOTA	4,657,758	76,044	4,360,889	65,814	4,295,075	128,056	56,934	111,879
MISSISSIPPI	2,716,115	20,149	1,702,058	15,988	1,686,070	986,895	9,638	17,524
MISSOURI	5,358,692	76,755	4,685,274	67,767	4,617,507	597,565	20,418	55,435
MONTANA	879,372	14,550	816,791	12,244	804,547	3,216	54,226	5,139
NEBRASKA	1,652,093	63,294	1,552,364	57,640	1,494,724	64,953	14,744	20,032
NEVADA	1,603,163	226,039	1,388,507	205,786	1,182,721	118,440	28,120	68,096
NEW HAMP-SHIRE	1,162,481	15,852	1,139,475	14,391	1,125,084	8,066	2,281	12,659
NEW JERSEY	7,987,933	920,085	6,414,926	792,965	5,621,961	1,157,171	20,622	395,214
NEW MEXICO	1,713,407	677,341	1,490,295	649,808	840,487	43,001	157,181	22,930
NEW YORK	18,184,774	2,537,597	13,991,765	1,916,575	12,075,190	3,198,235	72,963	921,811
NORTH CARO-LINA	7,322,870	134,384	5,518,807	114,871	5,403,936	1,624,259	93,963	85,841
NORTH DAKOTA	643,539	6,359	604,844	5,326	599,518	4,111	29,392	5,192
OHIO	11,172,782	168,711	9,766,839	149,373	9,617,466	1,264,493	22,356	119,094
OKLAHOMA	3,300,902	114,823	2,745,517	95,578	2,649,939	253,319	260,501	41,565
OREGON	3,203,735	177,233	3,005,721	162,308	2,843,413	57,752	44,116	96,146
PENNSYLVANIA	12,056,112	292,050	10,690,370	245,200	10,445,170	1,162,462	17,067	186,213
RHODE ISLAND	990,225	59,475	917,164	47,509	869,655	47,050	4,683	21,328
SOUTH CARO-LINA	3,698,746	40,771	2,543,890	33,747	2,510,143	1,115,869	8,754	30,233
SOUTH DAKOTA	732,405	7,266	666,157	5,782	660,375	4,542	57,221	4,485
TENNESSEE	5,319,654	52,302	4,385,463	44,667	4,340,796	874,592	11,843	47,756
TEXAS	19,128,261	5,503,372	16,203,786	5,309,635	10,894,151	2,336,165	90,035	498,275
UTAH	2,000,494	121,641	1,907,846	112,675	1,795,171	16,747	28,472	47,429
VERMONT	588,654	5,704	578,103	5,195	572,908	3,500	1,695	5,356
VIRGINIA	6,675,451	223,828	5,111,445	195,348	4,916,097	1,322,722	17,780	223,504
WASHINGTON	5,532,939	321,684	4,944,646	284,864	4,659,782	189,241	99,369	299,683
WEST VIRGINIA	1,825,754	9,892	1,756,915	8,790	1,748,125	57,600	2,544	8,695
WISCONSIN	5,159,795	122,622	4,756,004	109,880	4,646,124	284,368	45,277	74,146
WYOMING	481,400	27,536	463,029	25,578	437,451	4,082	10,558	3,731

Note: In the categories given above, American Indian includes Eskimo and Aleut

Source: Administrative Records and Methodology Research Branch—U.S. Bureau of the Census

5. Major Events in United States History

1700

1754 — French and Indian War

Boston Tea Party — 1773

1776 — Declaration of Independence

Slavery is illegal in Massachusetts — 1783

1789 — George Washington becomes President

Building of the White House starts — 1792

1800

— Federal government moves to Washington, D.C.

War of 1812 — 1812

1845 — Texas becomes a state

Gold discovered in California — 1848

1861 — Civil War begins

Lincoln frees the slaves — 1863

1865 — Civil War ends

1900

San Francisco earthquake — 1906

1917 — World War I begins

Word War II begins — 1941

1955 — Supreme Court orders school integration

President John F. Kennedy is killed — 1963

1968 — Martin Luther King, Jr. is killed

200th Anniversary of U.S. independence — 1976

1995 — Oklahoma City terrorist bombing

---

6. Weights and Measures, Temperatures (Celsius and Fahrenheit)

Weights and Measures

1 pound (lb.) = 453.6 grams (g.)
16 ounces (oz.) = 1 pound (lb.)
2,000 pounds (lb.) = 1 ton

1 inch (in. or ″) = 2.54 centimeters (cm.)
1 foot (ft. or ′) = 0.3048 meters (m.)
12 inches (12″) = 1 foot (1′)
3 feet (3′) = 1 yard (yd.)
1 mile = 5,280 feet (5,280′)

Temperature chart: Celsius and Fahrenheight

degrees (°) Celsius (C) = $\frac{5}{9}$ degrees Fahrenheight) − 32

degrees (°) Fahrenheight (C) = $\frac{9}{5}$ degrees Celsius) + 32

C:	100°	30°	25°	20°	15°	10°	5°	0°	−5°
F:	212°	86°	77°	68°	59°	50°	41°	32°	23°

7. Twenty Wealthiest People in the World

	NAME	COUNTRY	WEALTH ($U.S.)	SOURCE
1	Gates, William H. III	United States	51,000,000,000	Microsoft Corp.
2	Walton, Family	United States	48,000,000,000	Wal-Mart Stores
3	Bolkiah, Sultan Hassanal	Brunei	36,000,000,000	oil, gas
4	Buffett, Warren	United States	33,000,000,000	Berkshire Hathaway
5	Alsaud, King Faud Bin Abdul	Saudi Arabia	25,000,000,000	investments, real estate
6	Allen, Paul Gardner	United States	21,000,000,000	Microsoft Corp.
7	Al Nahyan, Sheikh Zayed Bin Sultan	United Arab Republic	15,000,000,000	oil, investments
8	Al-sabah, Sheikh Jaber Al-ahmed Al-jaber	Kuwait	15,000,000,000	oil, investments, real estate
9	Thomson, Kenneth	Canada	14,400,000,000	Thomson Corp.
10	Pritzker, Jay A. and Robert A.	United States	13,400,000,000	financiers
11	Mars, Forrest Edward Sr. and Family	United States	13,500,000,000	candy company
12	Alsaud, Prince Alwaleed Bin Talal	Saudi Arabia	13,300,000,000	investments, construction, banking
13	Lee Shau Kee	Hong Kong	12,700,000,000	real estate
14	Albrecht, Theo & Karl and family	Germany	11,700,000,000	retailing
15	Ballmer, Steven	United States	10,700,000,000	Microsoft Corp.
16	Mulliez, Gerard and family	France	10,300,000,000	retailing
17	Dell, Michael	United States	10,000,000,000	Dell Computer Corp.
18	Al-Maktoum, Makhtoum bin Rashid	Dubai	10,000,000,000	oil, services
19	Li Ka-shing	Hong Kong	10,000,000,000	real estate, telecommunication, etc.
20	Botin, Emilio and family	Spain	9,200,000,000	banking

8. Some Internet Usage Statistics

World Wide Web devices worldwide
(total # of computers accessing the web)
1997: 78,144,159
1998: 120,394,629

World Wide Web devices in U.S.
(total # of computers accessing the web)
1997: 49,381,480
1998: 72,143,711

World Wide Web users worldwide
(total # of users accesssing the web)
1997: 68,685,240
1998: 97,254,212

World Wide Web users in U.S.
(total # of users accessing the web)
1997: 38,739,864
1998: 51,594,024

World Wide Web pages
(total # of URLs worldwide)
1997: 351,010,467
1998: 829,429,194

Percent of computers and users on the World Wide Web
At the end of 1996, the U.S. accounted for 68% of the devices and 61% of the users accessing the World Wide Web.

Percent of U.S. households owing a PC.
At the end of 1997, 43% of U.S households owned a PC.

9. Immigration Patterns in California and Florida

Immigrants Admitted, by leading Country of Birth: 1995

FLORIDA
Total (includes other countries not shown here): 62,023
Cuba: 15,112
Dominican Republic: 2,090
Mexico: 1,922
Philippines: 1,806
Vietnam: 1,194
India: 1,141
Former Soviet Union: 1,021
China: 639

CALIFORNIA
Total (includes other countries not shown here): 166,482
Mexico: 34,416
Philippines: 22,584
Vietnam: 16,755
China: 10,256
Former Soviet Union: 10,045
India: 6,646
Cuba: 428
Dominican Republic: 71

10. Bicycle Owner-ship and Usage

- 90 million, or 46% of American adults ride a bicycle at least once a year.
- 500,000 Americans ride their bike to work.
- Nearly 80% of bicycle commuters are men.
- Roughly 70% of bicycle commuters are age 15-34.
- California has the highest percentage of bicycle commuters (13 metropolitan areas with at least 10 bicycle commuters per 1,000)
- Nearly 33 million Americans consider themselves recreational bicyclists.
- Recreational bicyclists are split equally between men and women.
- Four percent of recreational cyclists are black, with 2% Asian or other races.
- More than half of all recreational cyclists own air pumps, but fewer than half own locks and only 16% own helmets
- Nearly 40% of bicycle owner report having a mechanical problem in a given year.

Source: American Demographics

11. Non-English Speaking Americans

Language	1990 Population	1980 Population	Percent change
Non-English Total	31,844,979	23,711,574	34.3
Spanish	17,339,172	11,549,333	50.1
French	1,702,176	1,572,275	8.3
German	1,547,099	1,606,743	−3.7
Italian	1,308,648	1,633,279	−19.9
Chinese	1,249,213	631,737	97.7
Tagalog	843,251	451,962	86.6
Polish	723,483	826,150	−12.4
Korean	626,478	275,712	127.2
Vietnamese	507,069	203,268	149.5
Portuguese	429,860	361,101	19.0
Japanese	427,657	342,205	25.0
Greek	388,260	410,462	−5.4
Arabic	355,150	225,597	57.4
Hindi and related	331,484	129,968	155.1
Russian	241,798	174,623	38.5
Yiddish	213,064	320,380	−33.5
Thai	206,266	89,052	131.6
Persian	201,865	109,293	84.7
French Creole	187,658	24,885	654.1
Armenian	149,694	102,301	46.3
Navaho	148,530	123,169	20.6
Hungarian	147,902	180,083	−17.9

Note: Totals includes languages not shown here.

Language	1990 Population 5 years and over	1980 Population 3 years and over	Percent change
Hebrew	144,292	99,166	45.4
Dutch	142,684	146,429	−2.6
Mon−Khmer	127,441	16,417	676.3
Gujarathi	102,418	36,865	177.8
Ukrainian	96,568	122,300	−21.0
Czech	92,485	123,059	−24.8
Pennsylvania Dutch	83,525	68,202	22.5
Miao	81,877	16,189	405.8
Norwegian	80,723	113,227	−28.7
Slovak	80,388	87,941	−8.6
Swedish	77,511	100,886	−23.2
Serbocroatian	70,964	83,216	−14.7
Kru	65,848	24,506	168.7
Rumanian	65,265	32,502	100.8
Lithuanian	55,781	73,234	−23.8
Finnish	54,350	69,386	−21.7
Punjabi	50,005	19,298	159.1
Formosan	46,044	13,661	237.0
Croatian	45,206	42,479	6.4
Turkish	41,876	27,459	52.5

Source: 1997 Information Please (TM) Almanac

12. Slave Ownership in the United States

In 1861, Edward Dunbar, estimated that 14,000,000 Africans had been captured and sent to the Americas between 1500 and 1870.

In 1969, Philip Curtin published *The African Slave Trade: A Census*, in which he estimated 9,566,000 Africans had been sent to the Americas between 1451 and 1870. Below are the figures he arrived at:

prior to 1600	274,900
1600–1700	1,341,100
1701–1810	6,051,710
1811–1870	1,898,400

Curtin arrived at his figures by studying shipping and merchant records, as well as numerous other types of material that hadn't previously been studied. Later scholars claim that the number taken from Africa may be 12 million, or closer to Dunbar's figure of 14,000,000 because Curtin may not have accounted for the many Africans who died in capture or in transit. The actual numbers will never be known.

Source: Historical Encyclopedia of World Slavery, Junius P. Rodriguez, General Editor; ABL-CLIO

13. Irregular Past Tenses and Past Participles

Simple Form	Past	Past Participle
be	was, were	been
become	became	become
begin	began	begun
bite	bit	bitten
blow	blew	blown
break	broke	broken
bring	brought	brought
buy	bought	bought
cost	cost	cost
do	did	done
drink	drank	drunk
drive	drove	driven
feel	felt	felt
fit	fit	fit
fly	flew	flown
get	got	gotten
give	gave	given
go	went	gone
have	had	had
hide	hid	hidden
hit	hit	hit
know	knew	known
lay	laid	laid
let	let	let
lie (down)	lay	lain
lie (untruth)	lied	lied
pay	paid	paid
read	read	read
ride	rode	ridden
shut	shut	shut
steal	stole	stolen
take	took	taken
teach	taught	taught
wake	woke	woken
wear	wore	worn

14. Common Prefixes and Suffixes

Common Prefixes

Prefix	Meaning	Example
after-	after	aftertaste
ambi-	both	ambidextrous
anti-	against	antiwar
aqua-	water	aquarium
audi-	sound	auditorium
auto-	self	autobiography
bi-	two	bilingual
co-	with	cooperate
dis-	negative of	disappear
ex-	in the past	ex-wife
hemi-	half	hemisphere
im-	not	immature
inter-	between, among	international
intra-	within	intrastate
micro-	small	microscope
multi-	many	multiracial
non-	not	nonsense
post-	after	postwar
re-	again	remember
un-	not	unusual
zoo-	animal	zoology

Common Suffixes

Suffix	Meaning	Example
-an	belonging to	American
-arium	place, building	aquarium
-chrome	color	monochrome
-en	consisting of	wooden
-er	person who does an action	writer
-ese	relating to	Japanese
-est	most	biggest
-gram	written	telegram
-graph	written	autograph
-ion	process	communication
-meter	measuring device	speedometer
-ness	quality	rudeness
-phone	sound	telephone
-sphere	globelike	hemisphere
-ster	one who is	youngster
-ward	direction	backward
-wide	extent	worldwide

TEXT CREDITS

(Page 3) "Letter to Marilyn vos Savant." From *Parade Magazine*, August 10, 1997. Copyright © 1997.

(Page 7) "I Hear America Singing." Public Domain.

(Page 11) "Declaration of Independence." Public Domain.

(Page 15) "Second Inaugural Address of President William J. Clinton." Public Domain.

(Page 24) "Family Values and Reversed Worlds." From *The Time Bind* by Arlie Russell Hochschild, Copyright © 1997 by Arlie Russell Hochschild. Reprinted by permission of Henry Holt and Company.

(Page 29) "Homeless." From *Rachel and Her Children: Homeless Families in America* by Jonathan Kozol. Copyright © 1988 by Jonathan Kozol. Reprinted by permission of Crown Publishers, Inc.

(Page 34) "A Tale of Two Extremes." From *Personal Finance For Dummies*® by Eric Tyson, MBA. Copyright © 1994, 1995, 1996 Eric Tyson. All rights reserved. Reproduced by permission of IDG Books Worldwide, Inc. . . . For Dummies is a registered trademark of IDG Books Worldwide, Inc.

(Page 38) "Bill's $50 Bil: By All Accounts, A Lot of Dough." From *The Seattle Times*, April 23, 1998. Copyright © 1997, The Seattle Times Company.

(Page 47) "Kwanzaa History." From *Win95* Magazine. http:///www.win95mag.com. Copyright © 1996.

(Page 51) "The Gift of the Magi." Public Domain.

(Page 58) "Western Flyer." From *Reminisce*, July 1997. Copyright © 1997. Reprinted by permission of Reiman Publications.

(Page 70) "You Just Don't Understand." From *You Just Don't Understand*. Copyright © 1990 by Deborah Tannen, Ph.D. Reprinted by permission of William Morrow & Company, Inc.

(Page 73) "Mending Wall." From *The Poetry of Robert Frost*, edited by Edward Connery Lathem. Copyright 1958 by Robert Frost. Copyright 1967 by Lesley Frost Ballantine. Copyright 1930, 1939, © 1969 by Henry Holt & Company. Reprinted by permission of Henry Holt and Company, Inc.

(Page 78) "Vigilance." Copyright © 1997 Meg Cimino, as first published in *The Atlantic Monthly*. Reprinted by permission of the author.

(Page 79) "Fox Trot" Copyright by Universal Press Syndicate. Reprint by permission of Universal Press Syndicate. All rights reserved.

(Page 83) "Daddy Weirdest." From *Seventeen* magazine, August, 1994. Copyright © 1994, Rebecca Bary. Reprinted by permission of Writers house, LLC on behalf of Rebecca Barry.

(Page 91) "Searching for Gold Mountain." From *Journey to Gold Mountain*. Copyright © 1989 and 1994, Chelsea House Publishers.

(Page 95) "South Beach Seduction." By Stephen Dilaurio. From *The Miami Herald*, April 17, 1998. Numerous attempts have been made to obtain permission for reprint from the author, but permission has not yet been obtained as of press time.

(Page 105) "The Ties that Bind." From *Farm Journal*, May/June 1997. Copyright © 1997.

(Page 113) "Hand Gestures." From *Curious Customs* by Thadeus Tulja. Copyright © 1987 by The Stonesong Press, Inc. Reprinted by permission of Harmony Books, a division of Crown Publishers, Inc.

(Page 118) "ASL in America." From *Learning to See*. Copyright © 1997. Reprinted by permission of Gallaudet University Press.

(Page 123) "Speaking Different Languages." From *Men Are From Mars, Women Are From Venus* by John Gray. Copyright © 1992 by John Gray. Reprinted by permission of HarperCollins Publishers, Inc.

(Page 142) "Get Off Your Cusp and Live." From *Aunt Erma's Cope Book*. Copyright © 1979. Reprinted by permission.

(Page 147) "Roswell, New Mexico: Home of the Strange." From *USA Today*, May 23, 1997. Copyright © 1997, USA Today. Reprinted with permission.

(Page 159) "Old New Orleans." From *The First Book of Jazz*. Copyright © 1995. Reprinted by permission of Grolier Publishing.

(Page 170) "An Interview With Rebecca Lobo." From *NBC On Line: Golden Moments*. Copyright © 1996, The National Broadcasting Company. All rights reserved.

(Page 183) "Orwell Got it Wrong." By Michael Kinsley. From *Reader's Digest*, June 1997. Numerous attempts have been made to obtain permission for reprint from the author, but permission has not yet been obtained as of press time.